DEBORAH CLARKE

LIVE

YOUR

DREAM

Looking For That Elusive Something To Lead You To Success And Happiness?

LIVE YOUR DREAM
© 2017, by Deborah Clarke.
All Rights Reserved.
ISBN-13: 978-1532950032

Original Publication, September 1987
© 1987, by Deborah Clarke
Reprints 1991
Canadian Cataloguing In Publication Data
ISBN 0-921024-01-0

http://www.eBizCoach.ca

"I'd love to be your online personal success coach for the next 30 days. Check out my Live Your Dream Personal Success System below. Cheers!" Deborah Clarke
http://www.eBizCoach.ca/lyd-plus-success-package

TABLE OF CONTENTS

About the Author

Live Your Dream was first published in 1987, when Deborah was only 28 years old. Like you, she had experienced some success early in her life and career. Suddenly she found herself well established with all of her major goals caught up and she was left wondering what was next.

She tells the story:

'I was feeling like my life was being scripted like the end of a fairy-tale book when they write, '... and they lived happily ever after'. At that time I was only 26 years old! I knew I had to dig deep to figure out what success and happiness really meant to me. Writing Live Your Dream was therapeutic for me. It helped me to re-establish a plan of action for my life.

It will help you too!"

Deborah went on the road as a motivational speaker for a few years promoting her book. From her experience interacting with audiences and individuals she was able to develop a system that would go on to be the base of many of her formal training programs. This venture was long before the internet and online purchases. Imagine Deborah literally selling books from boxes in her travels. She also would take out small classified ads in the back of major magazines, people would see the ad, write out a cheque, put it in an envelope and mail it to Deborah. She would turn around and physically package and mail the book back to the new customer. She had clients all over the world, even then. She recalls some books going to the Caribbean, and even to Prisons. It was rewarding to have repeat customers, she recalls a father from British Columbia, Canada contacting her for a second book. He had purchased one for his older daughter and years later was wanting the same tools and exercises for his youngest daughter. In another instance a young man contacted Deborah, 12 years after the book was out of print, he had purchased the book from a 'garage sale' and he wanted to thank Deborah for the impact it was having on his life.

By 1994, Deborah returned to university and completed a professional accounting designation (CPA, CMA). She left her entrepreneurial roots behind and started working in a variety of finance and management level positions at a corporate level.

In 2001, the large oil company her husband worked for did a restructuring and cut out their middle management positions. The loss of a six figure income and pension was devastating for their family. Thankfully Deborah had continued to upgrade her skills and her education. She was soon able to replace the six figure income their family had lost and support both of their daughters through university.

'Family is everything to us. We knew we would do whatever was necessary to give our daughters the life and lifestyle they deserved."

The end of 2014 after a rewarding career helping thousands of students, (young graduates, internationally educated professionals and mid-life career changers) to start careers in business, Deborah retired and returned to her entrepreneurial roots.

In 2015, the original version of Live Your Dream was republished as an eBook on Amazon.

Clarke has formalized a step-by-step system for success and happiness that has helped her to live the life of her dreams. It's the same system and philosophies she has used to help thousands of people whose lives she has touched throughout her career.

Now 30 years later, in this new 2017 version of Live Your Dream, Deborah is making this proven success and happiness formula available to the masses. Now YOU can use it to find that 'elusive something' you are looking for to lead you to success and happiness too. Once read and learned, this book and the exercises within will become tools you can carry with you for life to help you get through the set-backs, obstacles and transitions you will experience in your life too. It's time to go for it – Live Your Dream!

Introduction

The Big Generation - Me

I, am part of a very big generation born between 1951 and 1966. We have already had a tremendous impact on society – opening schools as we entered them, causing a sudden need for more teachers, and then closing schools behind us as we left them. We also caused, what has become known as an 'echo-boom', with our children born in the years 1972 - 1992 (perhaps that is you reading this book now).

In 2017 my generation will range from ages 51-66. The youngest of us has entered our 50's and the oldest of us has hit the senior age of 65+. If you are one of the boomer children, *in 2017 you are likely to be in the age range 25-45. If you are Gen Z (<25)*

Echo Boom (Generation Y, + Z) = You

This book is written for you – the children of the baby boomers – Gen Y born in between 1972 and 1992 (ages 25-45) and the newer Gen Z (ages 24 and younger). Some group you together and call you The Millennials. While your parents are starting to stress over what's ahead for them, nearing or entering retirement, you are also entering a critical time in your lives. A time I referenced as "settling down years" in my first book, I'm noting as one of the first differences for you, generation Y & Z.

You are a generation that has been raised with 'change', you have learned to explore, innovate or adapt in almost every part of your life. "Settling down" has been postponed for many of you who are living the dream as individuals. You are exploring (or have explored) the world, which has become quite small. You are moving (or have moved) from city to city, find your way on your terms. So, while these 'settling down' years, defined as settling into one city, with one full-time job, with one partner and possibly children may be delayed, they are likely to still happen in the timeframe of your years 25-45. *While much changes between generations, much also stays the same.*

We like to think we're unique and unpredictable, but reality is we're more predictable than any of us care to admit.

So, back to those years, often referred to as our settling-down years or "family-oriented years". These are years when successful young entrepreneurs are less likely to take risks that may jeopardized the stability of their families. I know this to be true, because you are exactly where I was when I wrote this book the first time in 1987. I was 28 years old when the book was first published (long before the internet even existed). What is more relevant to you, is the transition place that I was at in my life, at the age of 28 – and I'm guessing you are in a similar place. Like you, I had achieved some success in my career and life, many of my lifetime goals were suddenly caught up. It was a stressful time for me, trying to decide what was next in my life. This book was therapy for me to Live My Dream … and I'm pleased to provide you with a revised edition today to help you (and remind you) to Live Your Dream too.

You, as Echo Boomers, must face this time period in your lives by strategically planning both your personal and business goals. Those of you willing to be assertive enough to take charge of your lives, (and your purchase of this book indicates to me that you are) will be the most likely to succeed.

So, this book is for you, a member of Generation Y or Z; but this book is also for people who are interested in taking charge of their lives – no matter what generation they come from. If you have a dream, it is never too early or too late to pursue it. I urge you not to abandon your dreams, but to read on and learn how to LIVE YOUR DREAM.

It's your turn – LIVE YOUR DREAM.

We all need to be Entrepreneurs

I consider all persons who are interested in the business of successful living to be entrepreneurs – at least at heart. Let me explain: the dictionary definition of entrepreneur is, "one who organizes, manages, and assumes the risk of a business or enterprise." We all understand the role of entrepreneurs in small business, but consider the word enterprise and its dictionary definition, "a project or undertaking which is difficult, complicated and risky." Doesn't that definition apply to life in general?

I consider life to be a big undertaking; it certainly is complicated and risky at the best of times. Right? If you consider yourself an entrepreneur by these definitions, then it seems to make more sense to approach this business of successful living by using the same strategies and drive that you would use for any business venture. As you systematically organize and manage your game-plan for life, you'll find it necessary to spend some time soul-searching and thinking about what lies ahead for you. This book will be a very helpful tool; after all, you are risking a lot – your happiness and fulfillment in life.

What's next for YOU?

Writing this book was therapy for me. I started writing it at a time in my life, career, when I felt all of my major goals had been fulfilled. A time when my goals had caught up with me ... and I was left pondering "what will be next". Now I ask, *"What's Next For You?"*

Transition Period

You will experience many "transition periods" in your life. I have often referred to these transition time periods as my "fresh out of school, can do anything" feeling. The first time most people relate to this "feeling" is when it comes time to leave high school and go on to college, university or work. What you need to understand is you will experience this same "feeling" many times in your life. We all do. Some transition periods require an in-depth self- assessment. So don't be too hard on yourself, it is okay to be where you are right now in your life. You will work through this 'transition' now, everyone experiences these feelings at some point and you will again and again throughout your life. What is different, is that our experiences happen at different times – so our transitions in life happen at different times. But what I have found, is these transitions do happen in a wide span but typically a similar time in most of our lives.

Satisfied but lacking for passion in Life?

Feelings of being satisfied but lacking passion for life, (or longing for more out of life) seem to be common to this time in your life. No-one is immune to these feelings, your social or economic level makes no difference. Somehow we have to realize what it is that we are really chasing in life. The only security we have is within ourselves.

A notable shift for this rewrite of Live Your Dream, is the increase of the number of people who share this feeling of being 'satisfied, but lacking passion for life'. I blame this on a social media syndrome, we are so connected today, we watch people post the happiest things going on in their lives and we compare ourselves. Without consciously thinking about it, we can't help but compare. It is absolutely essential that you live your own life, your way, not comparing – be thankful for the ability to stay in touch with family and friends through social media channels, but don't use it as a measure to compare. Understand pictures don't show the entire story, they are a fixed moment in time. While you may see happy smiling faces and good times, there may be something very lacking in the person, family, lives being depicted in the photo. Be thankful to be connected, but don't compare. *Work on making your own memories (shared or not).*

Happiness comes from With-in

This book will help you capture that elusive something which will lead you to success and happiness. It will help you to LIVE YOUR DREAM, or, perhaps more important – make your dream come true. It is my guess that many of you will find out after a lot of thought, (as I did) that your happiness must come from within. Once you find that inner happiness, the nagging need for something more in life will disappear. It is my goal with this book, to help you find that inner happiness, and with it, an inner peace.

POEM: Thinking

If you think you are beaten, you are;
if you think you dare not, you don't;
if you'd like to win but think you can't,
it's almost a cinch you won't.
If you think you'll lose, you're lost
for out in the world we find
Success begins with a fellow's will,
it's all in his state of mind.

If you think you're outclassed, you are;
you've got to think high to rise,
you've got to be sure of yourself before
you can ever win a prize.
Life's battles don't always go
to the stronger or faster man;
but sooner or later the man who wins
is the man who thinks he can.

- Written by Walter D Wintle.
- Remarkably little is known about Walter D. Wintle except that he was
a poet who lived in the late 19th and early 20th century - See more at:
http://allpoetry.com/poem/8624439-Thinking-by-Walter-D-
Wintle#sthash.93VD3zOO.dpuf

ATTITUDE

Chapter 1
Take Charge – Success Will Happen to You

Chapter 2
Problems and Choices

Chapter 3
No *NEW* Secrets for Success

Chapter 1

Take Charge – Success Will Happen To You

I'll never forget something that my brother, six years my junior, once said to me in my 20's. "You know what's good about you? You're out there running when everyone else is walking."

For the record, let's start with the dictionary definition of success:

Success – degree of measure of succeeding / a favorable termination of a venture / the attainment of wealth, favour or eminence. / one that succeeds.

Succeed – to turn out well / to attain a desired objective or end. Syn. – prosper, thrive, flourish.

Successful – resulting or terminating in success / gaining or having gained success.

Success has no gender. As you can see by the definition, there is no criteria for sex, age or marital-status in the definition of success. It can happen to anyone, at any time, at any age. Success has no gender, and most of all, it can (and will) happen to YOU. You make it happen.

I am a true believer of the idea that success means something different to everyone. Wouldn't life be boring if each person had the same criteria for success? Imagine everyone working in the same way, with no one leading, no promotions, no titles – everyone driving the same make of car – living in the same type of house – having the same views on all important matters in life. The reason our world is so wonderful to live in is that each person is so different; we all want different things out of life and there are successful people surrounding us in all areas of our lives. There isn't one definition of success, it's time to make your own luck and your own definition of success.

Before you can help other people throughout your life, you must help yourself. The days are long gone to be living someone else's dream, or to be waiting hand and foot on someone else at the expense of your own happiness and success. Your happiness and success in life has to start with a positive self-identity and healthy respect for who you are. It's true you have to love yourself first. No excuses.

Also gone are the days of leaving your life to chance, or doing well in your life because someone else believed in you. You need to believe in yourself. You need to make your own luck. *(Thankfully 'making your own luck' is exactly what we are going to help you with in this book.)*

Once you start 'making your own luck', your success and happiness will become contagious. You will start positively impacting the lives of many people around you.

When you discover ***an inner happiness, a contentment*** that you are living your life the way it will most positively impact you and everyone around you – you have discovered your 'super power'.

> Your super power is your unique fingerprint. You being you. Your success, is your story. It's your super power and your personal stories that make you interesting. Just you being you!

Option of making Choices

Success should see you doing exactly what you want to be doing, and the easiest way to be the best at what you are doing is to enjoy doing it. That all sounds easy and very basic, but unfortunately it isn't always that easy. More often than not people get themselves into positions which are other than what they wanted.

This happens for many reasons:

(a) **peer pressure** – doing something because someone else wants to see you do it;

(b) **confusion** – not knowing your real wants and needs;

(c) **the easy way out** – it didn't take any in-depth thought to get here.

We all have the option of making choices – yet some people don't exercise that option to benefit themselves – and again that is their choice. If you feel you are one of those people, you have already taken a step forward to overcome and change that. Believe it or not, the most successful people in the world "make" success happen to them. Others who aren't so successful sit back and just "let" life happen to them.

What keeps YOU motivated?

When asked at the age of 27, "What keeps you so motivated?" I explained that I had been writing out goals for myself for fifteen years; I had already seen a good majority of those goals materialize, many which I thought would take a lifetime to achieve. When your goals become real in your life, one by one, you can't help but be excited and motivated, ready to plan your next move. It's not writing out the goals that motivates me, it's seeing them become real that's motivating.

The Trick …

The trick to seeing our goals become reality is to set them in the first place. You'll never feel the same satisfaction if accomplishments happen by accident, or by someone else's planning.

So many opportunities are passed because you were unable to recognize them as opportunities. Soon you'll not only be able to capitalize on those opportunities, but you'll be able to create even more.

What does Success mean to you?

For several years during career week I spoke to one of our area secondary schools about setting goals. It has been a life-long objective to help young people realize they must take charge of their own lives; they must become responsible for themselves now, and in the future. For many of them it was the first time to be introduced to goal-setting.

The responses I would get were interesting. When I would ask what success means to them – quite often the general response goes like this. "I see myself 35 years old, career _____, kids, house, car, all the materialistic things …"

I remind these young people that in order to reach the age of 35 years old and have all these things they have to do something between now and then. Then I also remind them that they will have a lot of living to do after the age of 35. But the most important comment I have to make to them, and to you today, is

> You won't just wake up one day 'a successful person'.

Success is a journey … IT'S THE WAY YOU LIVE EVERY DAY OF YOUR LIFE. So time to enjoy, right?

What is Goal-setting?

A detailed list of your personal, career, and materialistic goals in life.

Personal	Career	Materialistic
Spiritual (inner/outer)	Career satisfaction	Financial Gain
Family goals	Business Growth	Material items
Physical/Health related	Professional Development	All money buys
Character traits	Financial rewards	

Your personal success and happiness will depend on you achieving a balance in all three areas.

Importance of Setting Goals

- helps you think about your future

- helps you to make wise choices

- helps you to recognize opportunity

- keeps you motivated, striving to be your best

- a good way to acknowledge your accomplishments

Exercise: Things I like to do

In order for you to put the passion, desire into anything, you must like what you are doing. Make a list of all of the things that you like to do. Eg. Hobbies? Types of clothes you like to wear? Hours you like to work? Hours you like to have to socialize/be with family? People you like to be around? Type of work you like (physical, mentally)? What interests do you have (sports, computers, cameras, video's, etc.)?
Make a list....

Things I like to do

-
-
-
-
-
-
-
-

We all have Choices

I want to help anyone who feels they are in a rut, to recognize we all have choices. What, where and who we are today are all due to choices we've made. If you don't like where your choices have taken you – change them! Today we call this 'mindset'. The great thing about 'mindset' is you can change it in an instant. You have 100% control over your thoughts.

Think of people you consider to be successful. Are they persons with a prestigious position – corporate or professional? Learn more about them – the city or district they live in, the kind of car they drive, the kind of home they live in, and everything you can learn about their lives in general. As I work with more and more people in senior, professional positions I've come to realize and appreciate how we're all the same. Real people.

Maybe you admire someone who always looks amazing, well dressed. By learning some simple imagery techniques you can look the same, and guess what they wear at home? Not too different from you I bet.

Remind yourself of a successful person or family from your home town, someone who seemed to have everything. Maybe he or she drove a sports car you always admired. What if you learned that same family has since split up, claimed bankruptcy, lost everything, except – of course – the luxury sports car (because it was leased).

Is that what success means to you? What I'm trying to do is have you picture the successful people you envy so much, and have you recognize they too are real people just like you and me. It's very possible the only difference between those people you put up on pedestals and yourself is their outlook on life, and the knowledge of what's important to them. Keep reading, you're going to learn a lot about yourself in the next few pages.

Never lose focus of what's most important to YOU

Success takes on a whole new meaning when you've witnessed someone else's misfortune, suddenly things that seemed so important become very minor. Ultimately, success should go hand-in-hand with happiness, and should not become so overpowering to you that you lose perspective of that. I'll add here once again,

> Success is simple. It's an inner happiness. What truly makes you happy inside?

You have to agree, successful people that surround you, in any field, all seem to have one common quality, they know where they are going. *At least it appears that way on the outside.* They appear **CONFIDENT**, sure of themselves and **CONTENT** with where they are in life and where they are going. They always seem to be one step ahead of the crowd.

You might be thinking of several people you know who are constantly reaching for the stars, yet continue to get nowhere and they don't ever seem content. Guess why?

1) They haven't acknowledged what makes them really happy (content inside), and
2) They likely don't have much of a plan or focus of where they are going.

What really matters to you?

Although there are sure to be deviations from your original plan, you must always remember what it is you are working towards and continue to strive in that general direction.

It doesn't do any good to start out like wild fire; if you are starting out in fifteen different directions – you'll end up going nowhere.

Many times I've had to sit down and refocus, or reevaluate, then start out again. If you are an ideas' person you will relate to that statement. Recognizing this need is key to keeping you moving forward in a pro-active, meaningful way.

If you start with your end goal in mind, you can find out how to systematically achieve that goal. If you never set an end goal (and several sub-goals along the way), you'll never get the satisfaction of achieving your goals set.

Lesson to remember:

You have to take charge of your life, presently and in the future, once you do – success will happen to you too!

Chapter 2

Problems and Choices

We, as human beings, each have the option of being someone different. Think of the poor little Brussel Sprout seedling who hasn't a chance of growing up to be corn, broccoli, or anything else other than a Brussel Sprout. That little Brussels Sprout seedling has a predetermined destiny – you don't, you can be whomever or whatever you want to be.

THE #1 CAUSE OF STRESS IS FEELING OUT OF CONTROL.

The many complexities of today's world, the demands we put on ourselves, as well as the demands of other people (whether parents, employers, partners, customers, associates, children) all contribute to the feeling of being out of control.

By the end of this book I hope you will have renewed faith that you can be the center of influence in your life. Outside concerns do not and should not be controlling you. It is when these outside concerns (which we usually have no control over) become larger than our center of influence (concerns that we do have control over) that we feel out of control.

It is essential we recognize that we are **responsible** . . .

"response-able"

We have *the ability* to choose *the response* to any situation. We are *"able"* to choose the *"response "* to any circumstance in our lives. Outside stimuli will always be there, we will be constantly challenged … but we will always be able to choose our response to the given situation. No one can take that choice away from us.

WE CANNOT SOLVE PROBLEMS USING THE SAME LEVEL OF THINKING WE WERE WHEN WE CREATED THEM.
- ALBERT EINSTEIN

CareersGettingStarted.com

We all have problems ...

If we were together in a room full of people and I set a bushel basket in the middle of the room asking each person to write on a piece of paper, a major problem they were having in their life and drop it in the basket, the results would be interesting. Everyone would be able to write something down on the piece of paper. If I were to mix these papers up and redistribute them to the group the feedback could also prove to be interesting.

- If the piece of paper you received had a problem of greater degree than your own, you would feel somewhat better. Maybe things aren't too bad you'd think.

- If the paper you received had a problem of a lesser degree than your own, you'd think to yourself, "he thinks he has problems, Ha." But at least you'd recognize that everyone has problems. All to varying degrees, but in the mind of the person who wrote the note, whatever it was, it was definitely a problem in his/her mind.

After the exercise, if all the papers were given back to their rightful owners and we had to review them to determine which was the most serious problem, we may be surprised to find the person in the room with the worst problem is not necessarily the person in the room with the worst attitude about life. A persons' attitude does not have to be directly related to the number of problems or concerns in his/her life.

A wise friend told me
something once that I will
never forget…

WE ALL HAVE PROBLEMS

WHAT MATTERS

IS HOW WE DEAL WITH THEM.

It's all how you look at things

What matters is the response we choose to solve our problems, how we look at things. You've likely been through exercises when you look at one picture and see two images.

The next page has a classic example:

What image do you see?

Do you see the young lady?

Do you see the old woman (witch-like character)?

Exercises like this have proven if we give you information in advance, we can affect what you will see or believe to be true. We can give two groups of people different information & predict which of the images they will see first.

The same happens in life every day. Different groups of people around us are given different pieces of information (input), and then often we end up in a room together to solve a similar problem (common output), chances are we will totally disagree with one another...because of the different pre-framing given to us. (If you've ever lived through a merger or acquisition, you'll know this to be true).

Yet each party can still be correct. There <u>can be two correct answers</u>. Once both sides are presented, the two parties may come to agree there are two correct answers. When this happens they will have experienced a shift of thinking. Only then you can get to the bottom of making the decision best for the established result required, or goal to be achieved.

Here is a great folk story that will allow you to experience the same 'shift' of thinking. (We call them paradigm shifts). Frank Koch told this story in Proceedings, the magazine of the Naval Institute, back in the '80's when I wrote my first "Live Your Dream" book:

Two battleships assigned to the training squadron had been at sea on maneuvers in heavy weather for several days. I was serving on the lead battleship and was on watch on the bridge as night fell.

The visibility was poor with patchy fog, so the captain remained on the bridge keeping an eye on all activities.

Shortly after dark, the lookout on the wing of the bridge reported "Light, bearing on the starboard bow."
"Is it steady or moving astern?" the captain called out.

Lookout replied, "Steady, captain," which meant we were on a dangerous collision course with that ship.

The captain then called to the signalman, "Signal that ship: We are on a collision course, advise you change course 20 degrees."

Back came a signal, "Advisable for you to change course 20 degrees."

The captain said, "Send, I'm a captain, change course 20 degrees."
"I'm a seaman second class," came the reply. "You had better change course 20 degrees."

By that time, the captain was furious. He spat out, "Send, I'm a battleship. Change course 20 degrees."

Back came the flashing light, "I'm a lighthouse."

We changed course.

The shift in thinking experienced by the captain – and by us as we read this account – puts the situation in a totally different light. We can see a reality that is superseded by his limited perception – a reality that is as critical for us to understand in our daily lives as it was for the captain in the fog.

Remember Einstein's quote from the beginning of the chapter. "Significant problems we face cannot be solved at the same level of thinking we were at when we created them."

Many successes are failures turned inside out

Don't consider any problem as a permanent deterrent to your life-long goals – instead realign your goals using the tragedy as a twist to overcome, consider yourself a more educated person having experienced the tragedy or setback in your life. Perhaps you can help someone else to avoid similar experience – perhaps you wish to just put the experience on a back shelf and move ahead.

Many of the greatest success stories come from people who have overcome tremendous setbacks, or have had to deal with major tragedy in their lives.

Keep an open mind is good advice as you approach life, and is also how you should approach the rest of this book while working through the exercises.

Be prepared for several "shifts" of thinking. Those

'aha' experiences are wonderful,

I believe we become better people with each and every aha we experience in life. Start paying attention to how often you experience an 'aha' moment or shift of thinking.

There is no mountain too high to climb, no challenge too great to conquer. Continue onward in your path to success, accept the fact;

> **<u>Set-backs will happen</u>**; as devastating as they seem at the time, you will overcome them, and you will learn by them.

You will become better and more experienced for them; and finally, your life will be richer and success will be sweeter. Many others have overcome tragedy, you will too.

Chapter 3

No NEW Secrets for Success

"You won't just wake up one day a successful person. Success is a journey – it's the way you live every single day of your life. Enjoy the journey."

There is more material on the market today about success, performance, winning than ever before. But if you go back and read some of the oldest books dated back to 1929 and compare the material with that on the market today, you'll find not much has changed. There are no new secrets. The basic message is still the same – and always will be.

There are two basic criteria for success:

-Make a decision to accomplish more

-Learn how.

Exercise:

Who is the most successful person YOU know?

I want you to *think of the most successful person you know*. Think of someone specific. (this was difficult for me to do the first time, and when I did decide on someone who I considered to be the most successful person I know, it surprised me ... take a minute and really think about who this person would be in your life. It makes you think about what you consider success.)

Once you have thought of someone. Write down the <u>qualities</u> and <u>characteristics</u> of that person that makes you feel he/she is so successful." "what is it about that person that makes you feel he/she is so successful?"

Try to think of 10-15 different qualities and characteristics.

-
-
-
-
-
-
-
-
-
-
-
-
-

Now go back through your list and see how many of these qualities are **"skills"** and how many are **"attitudes"**? Place an **A** beside those qualities and characteristics you believe are attitudes. Place a **S** beside those qualities and characteristics you believe are skills. There is no right or wrong answer, see how many A's or S's are on your list.

More attitudes or skills?

I have done this exercise hundreds of times in my workshops and only once have I had it backfire on me. The ATTITUDES always by far out-weigh the SKILLS.

We can talk about how important attitude is, but somehow this type of exercise hits home with the message. I am continually telling business owners and managers that if they bring someone into their business with a positive outlook or attitude, the necessary skills can be learned.

Reasons why people fail

Let me reverse the scenario for you. There are two reasons why people fail.

1) They don't have the CAPABILITIES
2) They don't have the PERSONALITY

The amazing part of this is that 87% of the people who fail do so because they don't have the PERSONALITY. They never seem to adjust, or can't cope with the circumstances.

Relate this same thinking to the SKILLS/ATTITUDES exercise you did just prior to this – in this last example what would the capabilities represent? (*skill*) What would the personality represent? (*attitude*)

Go right back to the basic criteria for success

1. Make a decision to accomplish more

    (*attitude*)

2. Learn how. (*skill*)

Let this information sink-in for a few seconds.

(Is this an 'aha' moment?)

No secrets just ATTITUDE and SKILLS

Everything you read or hear about success from now on you will be able to relate to this skill/attitude scenario. Athletes, business people, successful businesses, mission statements. Everything from now on – think that's the 'attitude' element and that's the 'skill' element. It works every time! Really!

YOU DON'T HAVE TO BE
GOOD TO START…

BUT

YOU HAVE TO START TO BE
GOOD

Success is the realization of pre-determined goals.

When you set goals for yourself, you become a success by achieving them. It's okay to achieve goals, then set them aside and move on to something else. It is also okay to change a goal before you achieve it.

Example:
-Early in my career a major goal was to supervise the travel agency I worked for.
-After that had been accomplished, I chose to reset my goal to own a business, one that I could own and operate while raising a family.
-I went ahead and purchased a business of my own and I successfully operated it for 3 years.
-Then as things changed in my life, (decision to move family homes and expand our family), I chose to sell my business and pursue an opportunity to fulfill another important goal.

You can set and reset goals, **don't be afraid to push the 'reset' button and move on with your life at any time**. You are in control of your goals.

Again I emphasize the importance of remaining flexible, and when working towards your goals, try to keep as many options open to you as possible.

Six P's for success

The following is a list of the six P's for success. As you read through each of these words and their meaning, try to think of businesses, people or other scenarios that you can relate to each word.

Passion
Purpose
Plan
Positive Attitude
Persistence
Power

The first in this guideline for all success strategies is

passion. Everything is so much easier and fun if you

have a passion for what you are doing. A passion is what makes you love to get up in the morning, and get to work early; it makes the day fly by, and has you staying up late just for the joy of it. It's what makes you love Monday mornings as much as Friday night. There is absolutely nothing that you can't 'do', 'be' or 'have', if you have the passion inside you to achieve that goal.

The second success strategy is **purpose**.

Sometimes I think of this as my 'WHY?' Why am I doing this? For major tasks, both in business, and in personal life, I'll sit down and write out three things – my primary motive, my secondary motive and other motives.

I find that understanding your true motives or your purpose for doing what you've set out to do will help to keep you on the right track; or it will make you realize that you've set out to do it for all the wrong reasons and possibly you will change your strategy.

Planning is what this book it all about. It is

imperative that with anything you set out to do, you realize that there is absolutely no substitute for preparation or planning in advance. Don't wander aimlessly through life.

Dreams and wishes are just that until you do one thing, and that is write it down. Once you do some research and write out your plans with action steps they become goals – a plan of all the things you want to do in your life.

Writing out your **personal plan*** in life is

every bit as important as writing out your business plan. Anyone who is currently in business knows the importance of having a well laid-out business plan. Or more simply put, when planning your next vacation, you'll soon realize the importance of a good road map to get you where you want to go. Don't blindly follow someone else's plan (a GPS), know where you are going. Have you ever gone the wrong way following a GPS? Yes. ☺ Know where you are going.

All of these things take planning – so do our lives. Ultimately we are each responsible for our own lives; it is up to no one else but us to ensure that we enjoy life to its fullest.

> *Yes! Planning! Get a FREE Copy of THE NEXT 10 REPORT http://thenext10.ebizcoach.ca to help you with your personal plan.

It's also true to achieve great success you need more than 'positive thinking'. You need to experience a 'positive feeling' about what you are about to do. You must be able to actually envision yourself doing what you have set out to do.

Close your eyes, picture yourself driving that new car, or sitting in the President's chair. What kind of picture do you see? Is it grey and dingy, or dark and faint? If it is dull then brighten it up, put some color in the picture, put a smile on your face as you envision YOU, yourself, doing whatever your vision is about. Picture every little detail in your mind. By doing this you are creating a 'positive feeling' about what you

have set out to do. In general, a **positive attitude**

and optimism will help you tremendously through life. Rather than seeing only the bad side of everything, look for the brighter side. For every negative thing you hear – think of a positive side to the statement or story. In the same light, with a positive attitude, you can find something good in everyone you meet. This is a lesson taught by my mother, who once said to me, (about her father, my grandfather): "You know, to this day I can honestly say, I've never heard him say a bad thing about anyone." He always seemed to find something good in everyone he ever met. There should, indeed, be more people like him in this world; perhaps, we ourselves can work towards this goal. People are far too quick to criticize, yet slow to compliment in today's society.

Looking for the good in everyone you meet is a lesson I've been taught over and over in my life, personally and in business. Try catching people doing things right!

STORY: In one business instance, I was working as a consultant on a productivity assessment for a company. I was observing an assembly line area of the business. Every morning the gardener who looked after the landscaping for the company would come by to say hello, and sometimes share a coffee with staff. When our firm met with the executive team to present our final report with the results of our assessment we met in a boardroom, and guess who was sitting around the table? Yes, the gardener ... turned out he was a retired doctor and now part owner of the company. His job on site was to look after the landscaping, but he was also part-owner of the company. Lesson learned: Never underestimate anyone. Look for the good in everyone you meet.

Be a fun person to be around

I can relate this back to my days in the travel industry. I was fortunate to do quite a lot of travelling during my six years in the industry, and one important observation I made was that those people who were well-travelled, seemed to enjoy every holiday. When something went wrong, if the hotel wasn't ready for them, or wasn't quite what they expected, they made the best of it and enjoyed their holiday anyway. I also observed the many who could do nothing but complain about their hotel, the flight, the meals, etc. and these people did nothing but ruin the holiday for themselves. I found that in all my travels you can indeed make the best of any situation – holidays are too short not to enjoy. So is life!

Wouldn't you agree life is too short not to make the best of it? People with a **positive attitude** and outlook on life are the most fun people to be around – are you one of those people?

There are no problems that there aren't solutions for. There isn't a goal you can set (if it's something you really desire) that you can't achieve.

One major accomplishment doesn't come along without several minor accomplishments along the way. Each is a stepping stone which will eventually pave your way to success. If you've planned each of those steps along the way, you'll be more than ready to conquer any obstacles which come up, and you will be ready to accept success and will enjoy it to its fullest when it arrives.

Problem-solving is something that comes to mind when I think of **persistence**. I can guarantee that there will be obstacles that you will have to overcome to achieve some of your goals. It is important that you tackle each of them with confidence and you overcome them – persistence is key.

When a major problem comes up, I have found this following method most effective in finding the solution.

Write out the problem. Sometimes just by writing it down makes it seem like less of a problem.
Write out all possible solutions to the problem, both positive solutions as well as the negative solutions.
Write out both the pros and cons to each solution.

Mark off which solutions you think to be most probable. If it isn't the solution that you favor, what can you do to alter the most probable solution?

If, through this analysis, you cannot come up with an acceptable solution to your problem, leave it for your subconscious to work on. Give yourself a deadline to mark the time when you'd like a suitable solution, then let your subconscious work on it for you. You have provided all of the information that your subconscious needs; forget about it for now, but be sure to recognize the solution when it comes to you.

Next Page:
*Work through the Done-for-you-tool: Problem-Solving Chart

YOU KNOW WHAT THEY

SAY ABOUT PROBLEMS-

"80% OF THE POPULATION

DOESN'T KNOW WE HAVE

THEM AND THE OTHER 20%

IS GLAD WE'VE GOT THEM."

Persistence and problem solving skills rank at the top of my list of key attributes when I reflect on past goal-setting experiences. Guaranteed, there will be obstacles for you to overcome. It is important that you tackle each of them with confidence – and overcome them.

Be persistent if something is important to you, don't give up and *YOU WILL* achieve your goals.

It's your life and you're worth it!

Problem solving chart

There will be obstacles that you will have to overcome to achieve some of your goals. It is important that you tackle each of them with confidence and you overcome them – persistence is a key word to success.

When a major problem comes up, I have found this following method most effective in finding the solution.

- Write out the problem. Sometimes just by writing it down makes it seem like less of a problem.

- Write out all possible solutions to the problem, both positive solutions as well as the negative solutions.

- Write out both the pros and cons to each solution.

Mark off which solutions you think to be most probable. If it isn't the solution that you favor, what can you do to alter the most probable solution? If you, through this analysis, cannot come up with an acceptable solution to your problem, leave it for your subconscious to work on. Give yourself a deadline to mark the time when you'd like a suitable solution, then let your subconscious work on it for you. You have provided all of the information that your subconscious needs; forget about it for now, but be sure to recognize the solution when it comes to you.

Problem (write it out):

_____

<u>Possible solution #1 (best/most favorable solution):</u>

_____

_____

_____

_____

<u>Pros</u>	<u>Cons</u>

Possible solution #2 (worst/least favorable solution)

_____

_____

_____

_____

Pros	Cons

Possible solution #3 (compromise/middle of the road solution)

_____

_____

_____

_____

Pros	Cons

OPPORTUNITY CHART

By setting goals for your personal and business/career success, you are better equipped and prepared to recognize opportunities when they come your way. So first recognize, then assess opportunities that come your way. Use this chart to assess the situation, to determine whether or not you will take advantage of the opportunity, whether it is an opportunity worth pursuing, OR is it an opportunity better left for someone else.

Opportunity

_____

_____

_____

Pros	Cons

Follow-up needed from you to pursue opportunity

_____

_____

_____

Further questions to have answered

_____

_____

_____

You will soon recognize a **power** in setting goals and achieving them. You'll recognize the power of the universe and the things around you. But there is a second power, a power of greater importance to you – the power that's inside you that will make you keep going. If you can grab onto that power, it will help you go anywhere or do anything that you want to do. It is the power that keeps you going when everything looks grim – a power that no one can teach you to find, but you must look for within yourself, for yourself, a power that will take you to all heights.

This leads me to a poem that is a favorite – the author is unknown.

Don't Quit

When things go wrong, as they sometimes will,
And the road you're trudging seems all uphill-
When funds are low and the debts are high,
You want to smile but you have to sigh-
When care is pressing you down a bit,
Rest if you must but just don't quit-
Life is queer with its twists and turns,
And every one of us sometimes learns
That many a man turns about,
When he would have won had he stuck it out-
Don't give up, though the pace seems slow.
You may succeed with one more blow-
Often good is nearer than it seems to a faint and faltering man-
Often the struggler has given up
When he might have captured the victor's cup,
And he learns too late as the night comes down,
How close he was to that golden crown-
Success is failure turned inside out.
The silver tint on the clouds of doubt,
And never can tell how close you are-
It may be near when it seems so far-
Stick to the fight when you're hardest hit-
It's when things seem worst that you must not quit.

Remember the impact of SKILL and ATTITUDE in ALL success.

Take a closer look - How many of the six P's are SKILL related and

how many are ATTITUDE related?

AWARENESS

Chapter 4
Discover What Success Really Means to YOU

Chapter 5
Choices

Chapter 6
Your Professional Image

Chapter 4

Discover What Success Really Means to YOU

If I give you a fish you'll eat for one day. If I teach you to fish, you'll always eat. -from the Bible

Before we go any further, I want to set one thing straight.

IT'S OKAY TO BE YOU!

Something I've learned over the years is that people 'at the top', people we put up on pedestals, are human just like the rest of us. As a matter of fact, that person at the top may even be you, admired by someone else. You see it is we, as outsiders, who want to see only the best in someone else's life. We make other so enviable, when really they probably, eat, sleep and live in much the same way as we do.

When looking from the outside-in, at people we admire and respect, we tend to see only the good and believe all of the myths, such as:

- never a troubled moment in his life
- she gets everything she wants
- he never has to try hard at anything

A friend of mine once said to a male colleague who was going through an identity crisis at a troubling time in his life. *"Show me a successful man and I'll show you a failure"*.

Another friend passed on a statement given to her by a wise business friend, which I'll always remember and cherish.

"Everyone has problems, what matters is how you deal with them."

This is a piece of advice well worth remembering, when we stumble upon troubling times in our lives we tend to feel we are the only persons in the world with problems – not so.

Remember, what matters is how we handle our problems.

If you really admire someone, or envy someone's position, why not study that person or position, and see what it is that you admire so much. Ask yourself why you couldn't be more like that person, or find out what background is needed to take on a position similar to the one you envy.

How? Why not call on that person (or someone in a similar position and ask for a 15-20 minute information interview? Most professional people really like talking about themselves, so you are likely to be granted the meeting. ☺

If it is important enough to you, you will do this. By checking further you will soon see both the good and the bad sides to the position or person's lifestyle, and once again you will realize that this admirable person really hasn't had success happen overnight and most likely hasn't had it happen without failures along the way.

More important, he/she has probably handled these failures in a way which has enhanced him/her as a person, and the failure has ultimately improved that person's business-making decisions and has helped to get him or her where he is today.

More often than not, these past failures seem quite small when we look back, comparing yesterday with today – and rightfully so.

People with the initiative, (that we all have) to take charge of their lives have nowhere else to go but up.

> It pleases me that you have taken the initiative to further improve yourself and your lifestyle.

I have made it my priority to enjoy life to its fullest and to help others to do the same. I get great pleasure in seeing others enjoying themselves – so much so that I find myself 'teary-eyed' over more happy occasions, than sad.

My philosophy is that life is much too short for unhappiness, so we had better enjoy it and make good use of every minute, hour, day that we are alive.

What I hope to do in this chapter is help you to recognize who you really are, possibly why you are that person, and who you'd rather be. If it sounds fairly straight forward and simple, it isn't. It is going to take a very open mind on your part, possibly some very painful thoughts, memories; most likely some things will come up that you hoped you'd never have to think about again, possible some memories you have never shared with anyone. You still keep them to yourself, but it is important for you to review them. Hopefully, after this exercise is finished you will have put your past behind you – forever.

It is important for you to be aware that you can be responsible for your own destiny and the earlier you realize this and start acting upon that thought, the earlier you'll start reaping the benefits. If not already, soon, you too, will be the envy of your family and friends as being the person who seems to get all the breaks.

So come with me, let's take that trip down memory lane. It will help you to understand the person you have become, and possibly *why* you have become that person. Once you have established that, you will be able to overcome any roadblocks that may be mentally standing in your path towards success.

The following parts of the chapter will help you determine where some of your insecurities and inhibitions have come from; and yes, we all have them.

Many times it is our subconscious which holds us back from doing things, and this happens without us even realizing it. Up until now you have probably had no control over those subconscious thoughts. Let me tell you something now that can change all of that.

Your subconscious works somewhat like a computer, it only understands what is programmed into it and has no power of reasoning to reject any particular thoughts – therefore whatever you repeatedly feed into it – it will believe.

Up until now, unfortunately, some of that programming may have been negative and until we change those thoughts they could be inhibiting you from performing at your fullest. Did you know that the average person can achieve 40-50 percent more than he/she thinks he can?

Think about your family background, how much influence has it had on your upbringing and your lifestyle? Both good and bad.

Take a few minutes now to answer, in your minds, the following questions.

Think of the personalities by whom you were surrounded, those who had direct influence on you: mother, father, aunts, uncles, grandparents, brothers, sisters, close friends.

Did you consider them successful people?

Did any of them support you in everything you wanted to do, or discourage you?

What attitude did they reflect to you about persons around you who were reaching out for success? Did they help you to feel positive about what those people were doing, or did they knock others' attempts for success?

Were they constantly striving for the better life, always starting something new, never seeming to follow through, or always striving for something better, but never with any real direction?

You can first answer these questions collectively about those with influence on your upbringing. But then I want you to think about each of those persons individually.

Ask yourself each of the same questions, applying them to each family member individually. You will recognize that one person may have influenced you in one way, while the next influenced you differently. You may never have thought of these people individually in this way.

A prime example is your parents. You may have believed that they influenced you jointly, in the same ways, yet each one may have instilled very different attitudes and ambitions within your subconscious.

Take a moment to jot down a few thoughts about these people and how they have influenced the person you have become.

Mother:

_____

_____

_____

_____

Father:

_____

_____

_____

_____

Grandmother(s):

_____

_____

_____

_____

Grandfather(s):

_____

_____

_____

_____

Brothers/Sisters:

_____

_____

_____

_____

Close Friends:

_____

_____

_____

_____

Past attitudes have a great bearing on your present thoughts and actions. There might be something that you may never consciously allow yourself to think about, but your subconscious will never let you forget.

Let me give you a tragic family experience as an example. (The important fact to remember here is a strong parent/daughter relationship.)

When my mother was a young girl of sixteen, she experienced a traumatic auto accident which put her into a coma and caused her mentality to return to infancy. It was indeed as though her life was starting over; she remembered nothing of her past or present when leaving the hospital. It was a very traumatic experience for everyone who knew her.

Nothing but the strong will and dedication of her loving parents and brothers, who couldn't stand to see their youngest child and only daughter/sister waste her life away, has made her the determined and completely open-minded woman she is today.

My grandparents wish never to have to relive that experience and when asked about it, they can best describe the trauma they went through by repeating what my mother's doctor told them: "This is something that your daughter will never remember, but also a time which you will never forget."

True as that statement is, (as my mother still remembers nothing of that dramatic time in her life), I'm convinced that her subconscious has never forgotten the time, effort, and drive that her parents instilled in her in order for her to recover and return to the real world as successfully as she has. The accident put her years behind her peers in school, but she continued on to business school and obtained an office job with her diploma, married and raised three healthy, happy, and successful children.

Then, after ending twenty-seven years of marriage and not working outside of the home, she moved out on her own, finished a nursing diploma at college and has continued to support herself for the past 30+ years. She is successful, independent and enjoying life to its fullest.

My point is – sixty years of determination, dedication and drive – where did all of that come from when she was so close to death at age sixteen and literally starting life over at that time? My only answer is her subconscious – and where did her subconscious get the message to make her want to continue life and handle any and all situations in an optimistic manner – you've got it – from her determined parents and family who trained her mind to think that way, and to never give up.

This is a situation where the subconscious had to be given a strong message for survival. You and I would have (hopefully) worked as hard as her parents did to ensure survival.

We all have this strong capability within us, so why not bring it out and work with it.

If you feel that you had a somewhat normal childhood (if there is such a thing) with no real peaks or valleys that you can relate to … then I urge you to look beyond that.

Think of your life today. Are there certain situations in which you feel less than comfortable? Do you allow yourself to be creative, or do you always have something inside you which says that's not really you? Do you experiment with things or does something inside you stop you and say that you are stepping outside your boundary, perhaps your comfort zone?

By studying situations when you feel uncomfortable, you can work backwards, and perhaps find out what earlier event caused your subconscious to place a barrier or restraint on you in certain situations.

I believe our subconscious is like a computer, constantly being programmed by one source or another. Unfortunately, like computers we are only as effective as the programmer makes us, and some programmers may have led our subconscious to believe we must work within a comfort zone and never step outside that barrier. What we must struggle towards is changing and working with the limits of our subconscious.

I have being doing this for years, it's possible, it's fun, and it's effective. Changing and working with the limits of your subconscious is an important tool to use when trying effective goal-setting.

Think about this: - we are all born to be winners, we are all born with a clean slate to work from. A child has no fear, a child does not know right from wrong. Those are things that are programmed for us.

Your subconscious will do absolutely anything you tell it because it has no power to determine right from wrong. Only what you tell it is right or wrong. Better yet, it cannot determine a dream from reality.

The problem you face as you read this, is your adult subconscious over the years, has already been programmed, if not by you, for you. What you must set out to do is change the thoughts that limit you and use a larger active part of your subconscious to assist you in achieving everything that is important to you. Make your subconscious work, as your personal computer, built-in to help you achieve your goals.

The mind is a much more complex item than either you or I will ever understand, but that shouldn't stop us from using it to the best of our ability.

Your mind controls your entire body, all of your thoughts about every given situation.

The magic of this is that you are not consciously aware of what you are thinking at all times … even during your sleep your subconscious is still working.

In some instances you probably already have it working for you, whether you realize it or not.

For example – have you ever put yourself in a position where you've tried to think of someone's name and can't right off the top of your head? So you say, "Just give me a moment, it will come to me." And like magic, it usually does, even though you are off talking and thinking about something else. You gave your subconscious something to work on for you, you forgot about it, and presto … a few minutes later it came up with the answer for you.

Imagine, your subconscious is like anything else, the more you use it the more effective it will be for you. The power of the mind is what few people ever take advantage of, although it's easy to recognize those who do put it to use.

It is possible, that not all successful people realize the impact that their subconscious has had on their success; but, if you think about some of these people whom you consider to be successful – isn't it clear that the one common quality that they possess is knowing what they want in life? These positive thoughts are the messages which have been directing their subconscious.

We can all send similar messages to our subconscious by goal-setting, effectively – to get what we want out of life. It is true though, that some of us will have to work a little bit harder to reach those goals because first we must determine what our goals are. But, we certainly can determine our goals, and it is never too late to work at it.

Once more I want you to think back to your childhood. This next exercise is an experience / strength chart which is one of the few ways you can have your subconscious start working for you, rather than secretively against you.

EXERCISE:

EXPERIENCE / STRENGTH CHART

All of us have had experiences which stand out in our minds. (They may not be anything you've ever discussed with anyone, but they have marked your memory of childhood for whatever reason or importance.)

Divide your page into two columns.

Label column one "Experiences"; then write out both good and bad experiences, memories that you've had in your life. Anything that stands out. Don't limit yourself, write out as many experiences as you can think of.

Label column two "Strengths"; you are going to write out the strengths that you have gained because of that particular experience in column one.

Example:

Experiences

1) Started working at age 12 part-time; bought my own roller skates.

2) Ridiculed in grade 5 because of crooked teeth – hated school, didn't want to go.

3) Vice president of students' council, prom queen in my grade 12 year at high school.

Strengths (Gained From The Experiences Above)

1) Ability to handle money; accept responsibility. My first independence.

2) Ability to stand up for myself. Proof you can live through bad times, and that good times follow.

3) Standing up in public, speaking and being accepted by others. Leadership; accept responsibility

Most of us hesitate to look back at past experiences because many that stand out in our minds may be things that were negative happenings at the time.

But it's important to look back, because while it may have had a tragic effect on our lives at the time, quite often a major strength is developed within us at the same time.

Once you recognize those strengths and learn to look to the positive benefits of those sore memories, then they are often cut loose from you, and your strengths can be used to your benefit.

Now write out the strengths that you see in three influential people in your life.   Eg. mother, father, older brother, sister, spouse, close friend, business associate

_____

_____

_____

_____

_____

_____

_____

_____

EXERCISE:

PERSONAL SUCCESS CHART

Think of all of the past successes you've had in your life. These do not have to be "earth shattering" successes, but anything that stands out in your mind as an achievement from your past.

List as many things in each age group as you can remember. If you need more space, use a separate piece of paper. This may be a good time to start a separate workbook for all of your life-planning strategies. I can't begin to tell you how many of these scribblers, or workbooks, I have filled over the years. As a matter of fact, this book is a result of all of those scribblers.

Age Group:	Success	Why Success?
5 - 15 years		
16 - 21 years		

22 - 29 years

30 – 39 years

40 – 49 years

50 + years

Most successful experience:

Least successful experience:

It is important to recognize the strengths in both ourselves and others around us. Before we go on to the next exercise I want you to write out your definition of success.

SUCCESS:

_____

_____

_____

_____

_____

Now list your most successful lifetime experience…and your least successful lifetime experience.

Most successful:

_____

_____

_____

_____

Least Successful:

_____

_____

_____

_____

_____

The purpose of the Personal Success Exercise is two-fold.

1) To have you recognize your past successes and to give some thought to these successes.

2) To *__determine the common qualities__* that each of your successes is based upon. For example: acceptance, power, recognition, independence, academic, achievement, monetary achievement, need to expand horizons, need for family acceptance...

List your top three successful qualities:

1) _____

2) _____

3) _____

While we are on the subject of our life span – this is how I summarized the life span in general (*when I was 26-28 years old*):

13 – 19 years	Precious teenage, self-discovery years
20 – 29 years	Growing 20's, learning years
30 – 39 years	Powerful 30's
40 – 49 years	Prosperous 40's
50 + years	The most enjoyable, relaxing and unrestricted years of your life.

[*as written verbatim by a 28 year old Deborah Clarke*]

"You may agree or disagree with my outline, but from the standpoint of a young lady in her late twenties', at a time of first writing, hoping to use all her learned abilities to make her 30's the most powerful years of her life, this is the way that I viewed (in general) the rest of the years of my life:

- seeing retirement in my early 50's (if there is such a thing as retirement by then). You may ask retirement from what? If you've been doing what you enjoy doing all your life, why would you want to stop or change that?

I guess that will be a whole new book in itself." [*end quote of 28 year old, Deborah*]

POST-SCRIPT NOTE: *Now, in 2017, in my 50's and recently retired from the corporate world I've been able to return to my entrepreneurial roots, two revelations are before me:*

1) *I was able to retire in my mid- 50's ... yahoo! Still love it when a good plan comes together.*

2) *I see the time from 50 – 75 as another very productive and profitable twenty-five year time span. Something I couldn't possibly have envisioned as the 28 year old I was when this book was first published.*

According to the former timeline presented, life was pretty much over by age 50. I recognize now, as a 28 year old that was as far as I could possibly see.

The former timeline presented also relates to the end of those so called 'settling down' years – where one is expected to live and provide for ones' family.

So, moving into this next 25 year span of my life is equally exciting. It will definitely be more on my terms, my way...with more leisure time for my husband and myself, my grown family, young grandchildren, my extended family and my friends.

When I reflect back on everything I have accomplished between 25-50 ... I can't help but be excited about what lays ahead for me in the next 25 years. But that my friends, is a whole different book – one of similar transition, but for your boomer parents' generation. ☺

Just recognize from this Post-Script ... skills developed now to handle transitions in your life will be used many times.

You have just completed a study of your past, a study which has hopefully helped you understand where you are coming from.

Hopefully you have recognized some important traits that have been inside of you looking for an out. It is so important that you feel good about yourself.

Much like the old cliché, "You have to love yourself before you can love someone else",

> You must portray confidence in yourself before you can expect someone else to feel confident in you.

Hopefully, the rehashing of your past has helped you to rid yourself of any burdens that you've been carrying, and this has highlighted your successes which you tend to forget or overlook as the years go by.

Now, anytime an experience from your past tries to hold you back I want you to *__focus on the strength__* you've gained because of the experience rather than the experience itself.

> WHY ARE YOU A BETTER PERSON FOR HAVING HAD THIS EXPERIENCE?

Part of being successful is having the ability to express your values. The next exercise will help you determine the values most important to you.

Several years ago I read the book **Success...YOU can make it happen** by Dr. Lila Swell; the exercise on the following page is an abbreviated form of her exercise on values. I enjoy sharing this exercise with others during my workshops and seminars. People are often surprised with the results, those who are not surprised will at least know their hearts and their heads are in the same place (as far as values are concerned).

For ease of measurement we will use the value of money to help us determine those values most important to us (although money cannot really buy any of these values).

EXERCISE: - <u>VALUES</u>

I am giving you a budget of $2,000.00, you may spend it on as many or as few items as you wish. You must spend all of your budget, but no more.

How will you spend your $2,000.00?

1. Rid the world of prejudice   _____

2. Serve the sick and needy   _____

3. Guarantee to be a famous figure   _____

4. Proposal to triple company earnings   _____

5. Daily massage, and meals by a chef   _____

6. Perfect insight to a perfect life   _____

7. Vaccine to stop all lying   _____

8. Set own working conditions   _____

9. Richest person in the world   _____

10. The Presidency/Prime Minister/Head of Government

     _____

11. Perfect love affair   _____

12. House with a view and favorite art   _____

13. Most attractive person in the world   _____

14. Live to be 100 years and never sick   _____

15. Free psychology visit with genius analyst_____

16. Complete library for private use   _____

17. Harmony with God   _____

18. Rid the world of unfairness   _____

19. Resources to donate $1,000,000.00 in gold to charity

          _____

20. Voted outstanding person of the year in all papers

          _____

21. Master any profession of your choice   _____

22. Time to enjoy yourself, all your needs and desires

          _____

23. To be the wisest person in the world   _____

24. Scheme an authentic serum in water supply – to rid the

    world of lies   _____

25. Ability to do your own thing no hassles _____

26. A room full of silver dollars   _____

27. Control the destiny of 500,000 people   _____

28. Love and admiration of the world   _____

29. Unlimited travel and tickets   _____

30. Total makeover, wardrobe and hair   _____

31. Membership at #1 health club   _____

32. Anti-hang up pill   _____

33. A computer for all facts ever wanted   _____

34. Unlimited amount of time for religion   _____

Turn to the next page once the $2,000.00 budget is spent.

Add up the dollar values corresponding to the numbers.

$$ Value	Item #	Value
_____	1 and 18	Justice
_____	2 and 19	Humanitarianism
_____	3 and 20	Recognition
_____	4 and 21	Achievement
_____	5 and 22	Pleasure
_____	6 and 23	Wisdom
_____	7 and 24	Honesty
_____	8 and 25	Autonomy (freedom)
_____	9 and 26	Economic
_____	10 and 27	Power
_____	11 and 28	Love
_____	12 and 29	Aesthetics
_____	13 and 30	Physical beauty
_____	14 and 31	Health
_____	15 and 32	Emotional well being
_____	16 and 33	Knowledge
_____	17 and 34	Religion and faith

Judging by the highest dollar value spent – where do your true values lie?

List your top three values, and what each of those values means to you.

TOP THREE VALUES

1) _____

_____

2) _____

_____

3) _____

_____

*NOTE: I would like to add here that I have completed this exercise many times over the years. My #1 value hasn't varied, but values #2 and #3 have altered depending on where my focus in life has been at that particular time. Keep this in mind and try the exercise again in six months to one year.

Success is something that is bred from within – it starts with an infant at birth and continues growing within us until death.

Success is very personal; it can mean something different to each of us, the important thing for you to understand is what success means to you.

Don't waste your time or energy on things that you will never achieve simply because they don't really matter to you, that thinking is self-defeating.

In other words, don't continue striving to achieve something your parents, partner or friends want you to achieve; concentrate on what you yourself want to achieve.

There may be a difference; if there is, recognize it and change it. Only you really know what success means to you –

Go ahead, be successful;

Live your dream!

Chapter 5

Choices

You are entitled to live your life as you wish – just be sure what you are wishing is the way you really want to live.

With the past all behind us I want you to start thinking about the things you'd like to work on changing. What about thoughts, ambitions you'd like to feed into that subconscious computer of yours. We often live at such a busy pace that we don't even take the time to see if we're still headed in the direction we want to go.

My objective with this book has been to provide you with the step by step information necessary to help you clear the path towards your goals, perhaps finding a more direct route than you expected, allowing you to enjoy life to its fullest along the way.

> In today's fast-paced society, we need the assistance of someone to make us sit back and take a good, hard, look at ourselves and our lives to determine what we want out of life, and whether or not we're actually working in that direction.

Some people will be surprised that they're working in the opposite direction, backing themselves into a corner.

Someone very close to me, during a crisis time in the family, said "Deb, I've spent all of my life managing someone else's budget, books and prosperity to ensure his success in business, I never stopped to assess what I really had myself, as a person, as a family."

Somehow, it's only after it's too late that so many realize that their own personal lives take some managing too. And – life can't be taken for granted, as many people do.

I'm sure that we, at some point in our lives, have found ourselves working endlessly, without a spare moment for our own personal enjoyment, and unable to share our family's enjoyment. We can only stop and wonder – why? Why am I working so hard, if I can't even enjoy what I have now?

Take time to appreciate what you already have

This puts me in mind of another scenario, my own wedding reception. My husband and I are from rural Ontario, Canada and the dance part of the evening was open to all family and friends, with or without invitation. Because of the large crowds of people usually in attendance to help celebrate such an occasion, it is operated as a cash bar usually from 9:00pm – 1:00am.

Prior to our wedding day I was given a bit of advice from a friend who had just been through her 'big' day. Her advice was - '*take a few minutes just to sit down, by yourself, and watch what is going on around you.* The night goes by so fast; you see, talk and dance with so many people that the next day you can hardly remember what happened."

Her advice hit home and in the midst of the busy evening I took five minutes to sit down and do just that – view the crowd of over 650 people who had gathered to dance, visit and celebrate with me, my husband and our families. Still to this day eight years later *[now 37 years later ☺]*, that five minute pause is the clearest memory I have of the entire day.

My point is that life could be viewed in the same manner. I can't stress to you enough the importance of taking time out to just sit back and view and enjoy what you already have, otherwise, life will pass you by so quickly, as did my wedding reception, you will hardly have any memory of what happened. By taking a few minutes now to view your current lifestyle and personality, you will get a clear picture of

What is it you like about your current situation?

and 'what would you like to change?'. Most of all, it will help to keep you on track, to recognize what you already have and perhaps what you really want; then, when you achieve any further goals you will also recognize them and will be able to take five minutes out to enjoy their reality before continuing on.

A Great Folk Story ... about a man who has died and whose soul has gone to the gates of heaven.

> God asks him, "What do you think your destiny should be, my son?"
>
> The man replies, "Well God, I think I should go to heaven. I have worked very hard all of my life. I have toiled and slaved and worked unceasingly. My whole life was filled with work. I did what you wanted me to do. If I do not deserve heaven, God, then who does?"
>
> God looked gently at the man and then, with great kindness, said, "Yes, my son, you did work, but you did not have time to appreciate my sunsets, to stand in awe of spring, to smell my flowers, or enjoy any of the delights that I have made for you. You want to enter my paradise in heaven, but you did not enjoy the paradise I had created for you on earth."

Stop and smell the roses

I am a true believer of the importance of 'stopping to smell the roses along the way." Life goes by too quickly; while I want to be remembered as having left some impact on society after I'm gone, I also want to be remembered as someone who would take time out to enjoy the beauty of her surroundings, family and friends.

We all have choices

We wouldn't be who, what, where we are today without the choices we have made thus far. I would like to share with you some research I've done. In order to have you determine whether you are 'proactive' or 'reactive' in choosing your response to a given situation. Consider this …

"It's your responsibility"

My mother has tremendous patience and is a wonderful disciplinary. After spending a few days with my two daughters who were ages 6 and 4 [now 30 and 32], trying to teach them responsibility, my youngest daughter loved catching me not putting something away, so she could sing out "Mom, it's your responsibility". Their grandma had taught them well, the meaning of 'responsibility' … she was trying to get the girls to be proactive in their decision making processes … singing out, "it's your responsibility" each time she came across something she thought the girls should be doing, or cleaning up.

I've researched this further ... the word 'responsibility' can be broken down into two words to send us an important message.

RESPONSIBILITY

"response – ability",

the ability to choose your response to any given situation.

It's not what happens to us,

but how we respond to what happens to us that hurts us.

This is most important for us to remember when something 'bad' happens to us. Without exception bad things will happen to you from time to time throughout your life.

Remembering this word 'response-ability' will remind you, that you do have the ability to choose your response to what just happened to you.

Whether good or bad, you have the ability to choose your response, and that choice in the end will say more about you – will reflect on you and your future, more than what actually happened. Re-read this, these are words worth remembering...

24 Hour Rule

A rule that I've adopted in my businesses, corporate career leading people, and with my family is a 24 hour rule. If someone says or does something I don't like you can rest assured I will be letting you know within 24 hours.

The reverse is the same I ask of you – If I do something, or say something you don't like you have 24 hours to tell me.

The last thing I want is small problems brewing to become mountain size problems. If you are proactive and deal with problems as they happen it is best for all involved. Now, having said this, I do give most situations 'time', so rather than being reactive to the situation, I am likely to give it some time, in order to diffuse some of the angst and properly think through a suitable response. Thus the importance of the 24 hour rule, give yourself some time, but keep it within 24 hours whenever possible to let your feelings be known.

RECOMMENDED READING: "The 7 Habits of Highly Effective People" by Stephen Covey (Fireside/Simon and Schuster)

AAA Personal Success Formula

ATTITUDE + AWARENESS + ACTION

You are half way through this book, You are living out another theory of mine. You are being proactive, rather than reactive. Throughout your life thinking in the terms of this formula Attitude + Awareness + Action = Personal Success, will take you far. Let me explain how attitude, awareness and action will influence every decision you make:

ATTITUDE [choosing how you look at everything]

Absolutely everything you do is influenced by your attitude. It is quite simply the single most important factor in determining your success or failure. Attitude influences your outlook on life and every situation that will happen to you in your life. This should be the base 'check-point' for you in all decisions to be proactive.

AWARENESS [acquiring your skills, knowledge and resources]

But, attitude alone is not enough. We all have limitations, and must act responsible, be knowledgeable enough to make choices that will enhance our being, not hinder it. This is where awareness comes into play. It is the step that allows you to 'learn how', find out what you need to know to make wise choices and solid decisions.

You have walked through important awareness exercises in chapter 3:

*You discovered what success really means to you.

*Your most predominant strengths, qualities and values.

*Earlier in this chapter I hope you've been able to identify with the difference between being 'proactive' vs 'reactive' in your response to given situations.

In chapter six, I want to make you aware of how you can further enhance your likelihood to succeed by using external influences to your best advantage.

ACTION [taking steps forward]

Attitude and Awareness are key elements in preparing yourself for success, but nothing will happen until you put this information into ACTION.

Chapters seven through ten will provide you with concrete exercises, theory and practical application to do just that, GO FOR IT.

Chapter 6

Your Professional Image

- **Become the Right Person**

- **Visual Image**

- **Developing Charisma**

What you are speaks so loudly, I hardly hear a word you are saying.

By the end of this workbook, you will have established a set of written goals, in this chapter I want to make you aware of the external powers of influence available to you to make your goals attainable.

Once your goals are established your subconscious will take charge and help you work towards these goals without you even being aware this is happening. But there are also external influences you can take advantage of to assist your subconscious to achieve your goals. You have to become an 'opportunist', one who can and will take advantage of opportunities as they arise for you, and in order to do so you must first be capable of recognizing those opportunities as such.

While you will be amazed at how 'all of a sudden these opportunities arise for you', setbacks are also sure to occur. Obstacles can, and will, be overcome. Life goes on.

This is where optimism comes in, and it is also very important for you. There is certainly nothing wrong with admitting a mistake; we all make them and generally, if acknowledged in the proper context, we become better for them. There is truth to the statement 'we learn from our mistakes'. You should acknowledge and analyze your mistake – think about what has been learned by your mistake and retain that information for the future so that mistake isn't made again.

Setbacks WILL Happen, Experience is Still the Best Teacher

"Experience is the best teacher", is a common cliché. Those who are afraid to go out and truly experience life, must learn they are sheltering themselves from the life they now only dream about happening.

That life can, and will, begin happening if they will only set aside those fears, go out with optimism, and understand that setbacks will happen; you'll overcome them, learn by them, become better and more experienced for them; your life will be richer and you'll continue on your path to success.

Success, happiness, and fulfillment are seldom handed to anyone, but at the same time they often take less effort than what you'd imagine.

An interesting survey of seniors over the age of 90 years, asked them what they would do differently if they were to live life over. A similar response came from the majority of those surveyed.

THEY'D TAKE MORE RISKS!

Imagine yourself at the age of 90. What will you be happy with having accomplished in your life? Think about it now … don't have any regrets.

The following poem, author unknown, points out that we all risk something every day.

RISK

To laugh is to risk appearing the fool
To weep is to risk appearing sentimental
To reach out for another is to risk involvement
To expose feelings is to risk exposing your true self
To place your ideas, your dreams, before the crowd is to risk
their loss
To love is to risk not being loved in return
To live is to risk dying
To hope is to risk despair
To try is to risk failure.
But risks must be taken, because the greatest hazard in life is
to risk nothing.
The person who risks nothing, does nothing, has nothing and
is nothing.
He may avoid suffering and sorrow,
But he simply cannot learn, feel, change, grow, love, life.
Chained by his certitudes, he is a slave.
He has forfeited his freedom.
Only a person who risks … is free!

EXERCISE(S):
How to Create Opportunities for Yourself

Once you know and understand: 1) what you want to achieve, and 2) how you would react to a given situation things often have a funny way of just turning out "lucky".

Pointer #1

"Success Breeds Success"

- Surround yourself with as many successful people as possible

- Do you belong to any type of networking group?

- Do you belong to a professional association?

- Do you belong to any other community, civic, or hobby group?

If you answered no to any or all of the above questions, I strongly suggest and urge you to come out of your shell and find out more about these interest groups. You can get a list of all of the organizations in your area, for a nominal fee, through your local Chamber of Commerce office. Contact them today; you'll be surprised at the number of groups that will interest you that you didn't even know existed.

Pointer #2

List five people with whom you'd like to increase or renew connections:
1)
2)
3)
4)
5)

Pointer #3

List five people you serve as a role model or whom you should be bringing along in their life or careers.
1)
2)
3)
4)
5)

Pointer #4

"Once you are prepared, circumstances have a way of turning out lucky."
I call this my elevator exercise; I use it often: Imagine that you have just stepped into an elevator with your boss's boss, or someone very influential to your career or your getting ahead. You are going to be alone for the next 30 seconds. What would you say to that person to position and connect yourself as well as possible? Be specific.

You will probably find yourself using the 'elevator exercise' over and over again as I have – it is effective and better yet, it works.

Networking – people helping people – it works!

"Networking" was quite a trendy word in the 80's when I first wrote this book, as a 28 year old. Not only has it continued to be an important skill to learn, I feel very confident saying it is the #1 way new grads and career movers get jobs.

Some people are intimidated by the very thought of formal networking groups. Don't be, simply put networking is people helping people. We need to rid ourselves of 'past thinking' that if I'm to win, you must lose.

We need to concentrate our thoughts on 'win-win' situations. Remember success breeds success, winners surround themselves with winners. Surround yourself with as many successful people as possible.

Many Benefits from Networking

The benefits of networking are many. If you are not already aware of what formal networking is all about, you had better read along very carefully; networking can make your life a lot more enjoyable and you will be surprised at how easy it really is to get what you want, when you know the right person/contact.

> You've heard the old cliché, "Being at the right place, at the right time."

This statement is definitely right on track with the way things go; we've all seen it – I know that I certainly have. It's likely that you have, too. The trick to this is becoming the person who is at the right place at the right time. This is where networking comes in nicely.

Networking in the formal sense of the word is a term used when a group of people get together to share experiences, support one another's endeavors and to establish business and government contacts.

Networking is also effective on an informal basis and has been happening for years. Often referred to as "the old boys networks", men have been sharing business experiences and gaining new business contacts through many a golf game, lunch, and locker room experience, etc.

Business women realizing those "locker room" situations don't come along easily, started formalizing business women networks. It was indeed an important part of my business growth being associated with a strong Business Women's Network. I was only 24 years old when I joined my first formal business network. There was an interview process to be accepted into the group – these successful business women watched me grow up, and many words of wisdom that I've carried with me through life came from these influential women.

There are about as many different networking groups as there are different types of people, I strongly advise you connect yourself with a business group related to your area of expertise or interest.

Some groups are labeled as networking groups, while others are simply interest groups, or hobby groups, or charitable groups, or professional associations. Call them what you like – the connections are still there and if you share the same interests as others in your group (and of course you do, that is why you joined) you'll find doors opening for you when help or assistance is needed.

Seek out local groups and organizations through your local Chamber of Commerce or Board of Trade. Most Chambers keep a list of all of the clubs and organizations in your area with the contact names and phone numbers for further information. I urge you to join any group that may be of interest to you.

If you don't feel there are any existing groups attracting the people that you would like to 'rub elbows with', look into starting up a group of your own. Chances are good there are other people like you out there, just waiting for the same opportunity.

Quite often formal networking groups have a criteria that you must meet.

For example
– A business women's network would obviously be women in the business world, women who are possibly working at different capacities or women in upper management levels;

-A business owners' network could be available for male and female business owners. This would be a beneficial place for people to compare notes, government policies affecting small business, etc.

All of these types of groups keep you informed about trends, current events, and they often open doors for you when you have a task at hand to accomplish.

Social Media has brought a whole new realm of networking groups and opportunities. LinkedIn and Facebook Groups are a good way to get started to collaborate with persons of similar interests.

But, I can't stress enough, the value of face-to-face networking or information seeking. Get out and meet people, join a group that meets face-to-face, at least occasionally.

Check out my career blog – for an article about the importance of finding "Stretch People" in your life.

Blog: (search "Stretch People" keywords)
http://www.CareersGettingStarted.com
Like Our Facebook Page So You Never Miss A Thing:
http://www.fb.com/CareersGettingStarted

Networking Meetings

Formal Networking Groups typically have monthly meetings – either over lunch or dinner – with the business portion of the meeting following the meal. This allows for informal networking to occur during the meal, often speakers of interest to the group are brought in following the business part of the meeting, and this provides further interest and educational topics for the members.

Currently I belong to an International Association of Women in Coaching. The group has its' own business website, private members area, private Facebook Group page for member interaction and we meet one or two times a year in Arizona. Women from all over the world belong to this group – as our global boundaries expand, so do our networks.

We need these types of groups to continue growing and developing in outlying areas, in major city centers, nationally and internationally. Networking is an important asset to anyone, but especially to those in the business world who may not otherwise have a large "contact base" outside their own business associates. Many of these networking groups don't involve a lot of time on the members' part (other than the monthly meeting) yet they provide a wealth of stimulation and opportunity for the members.

Your life deserves the reassurance offered by associating with like-minded individuals. Reach out for the helping hands awaiting you, and perhaps you can assist someone else at the same time.

Information Meetings

I have witnessed the benefit of strong networks first-hand. Not only has networking helped me to secure some of the great positions I've landed. In my most recent career helping business students' transition into their careers in business and accounting, networking was the #1 way new grads were getting jobs.

So much so, I began advocating 'information interviews'. Advising students to seek out someone with the position they would like to have, or someone working for the company they would like to work, or someone in the same profession they are interested in pursuing. Find out someone you might be able to meet with, contact them and ask for a 15-20 minute meeting to talk to them about their career.

Your goal in this 15-20 minute meeting,

'just to get them to like you.'

How do you do this? Use a technique I call the 'likeability factor'. When people like you they will talk about you, they will want to do you a favor, or help you. So to prepare for your meeting, your focus should be 'what can I do to get this person to like me?' Can you think of some ways to do this?

Here are a few techniques:

1) Be prompt, on time (5 minutes early is perfect);

2) Be prepared, have some questions ready to ask, know something about the company or profession already;

3) The number one way to assure your 'likeability' status … is to be prepared with questions you can ask about them personally. Ask where they went to school, or got their education – or what was their first job like – or how did they get started with the company they are with now – or if they had to do it all over again would they pursue this career path – or if in your shoes, what would they do differently this time? Anything that will get them talking about themselves.

The #1 way to get someone to like you, is to get them talking about themselves.

I can guarantee, when you leave the meeting, they will be thinking, wow that was a great kid or young man, or young lady ... and if opportunity presents itself (either directly with his/her company or when talking with someone within his/her network), you will be remembered. ☺

Effective Communications

You are your own public relations department

Whether you realize it or not, public relations is an important part of people's lives.

Business owners use effective public relations to enhance their credibility in the eye of the community;

Corporate people use public relations to promote the positive effects of their company to society;

Career-minded individuals use effective public relations to become well enough known and respected in their field that promotions may come more easily;

Students use public relations to 'win over' teachers, and to win student body elections, then to win over the participation of other students;

School and the community; clubs and organizations use effective public relations to recruit volunteers for their groups and to raise public awareness of their purpose.

So you can see that public relations is something that should not be ignored by any of us. It is something that can be used to assist us to get what we want, possibly faster than you might expect.

Like anything else worthwhile, establishing public relations skills must be practices. It is something that is used by everyone at some point in his/her life; the key is to know when to use it, and how to use it to benefit you the most.

Tips to achieve power and influence

Take inventory of yourself and your habits:

Are you always on time, or can others count on adding ten minutes leeway for your appointments? What does this do for your reliability?

Are you always well prepared? Business people don't like surprises.

Can you always be counted on to come through when necessary?

Are you moody? On top of the world one moment or one day, then in the dumps the next? Again, reliability is the factor. People want to know that they can depend on you.

Step out of your body for a moment and take a look at what you see. More importantly, look at what others see when they look at you. Are you impressed with what you've viewed? If not, start making a list of constructive changes.

Listen to yourself when you speak to other people. If you sound unsure of yourself when speaking, or if you find yourself babbling, maybe you should sit back and listen for a while, then speak only when you have something worthwhile to contribute to the conversation – something which won't have others questioning your credibility.

In other words be comfortable speaking in front of others, but get your facts and stories straight first. While no one likes an air brain, (who blows off at the mouth), it's equally important to get noticed in order to get ahead, and you don't get noticed sitting back in your chair, never being heard from.

Be an Effective Listener

Being an effective listener is a must when you are talking over the telephone. You often have to listen between the lines in order to understand what the caller is saying when you can't see any gestures that may help you when speaking in person.

You may be speaking to someone who falls into one of two categories of telephone users –

Those who use the telephone most efficiently, he or she will come across with authority and influence. Don't waste his time, get the facts and points straight and then end the conversation.

Those who are quite uncomfortable using the telephone. This person may be wonderful to talk to one-on-one, showing confidence and good presence in most situations, but something happens when he/she picks up the telephone in business – uh, um, ok, ah, rambling on with way too much background information, then quite often hangs up without getting all the information needed.

If you're talking to the second type of telephone user you must really listen between the lines, better yet, you'd benefit by taking control of the conversation, getting out of it what information you need by asking the questions or by explaining your service or product in full rather than waiting for her to ask all the right questions.

In both of my first two careers, in the travel industry and the maid service I owned, using the telephone effectively was an area which allowed no mediocrity. Today as a business coach, I need to listen effectively and often need to take control of the conversation by asking – without any further information 'what is your question?'

> Be clear upfront, if someone doesn't know what you are asking of them, they don't know what to be listening for to help you .

With my maid service [pre-internet], approximately 95% of our business was confirmed over the telephone. My advice to the person taking the incoming calls was:

Have a pen and paper handy at all times to jot down important notes while speaking to the customer. Jot down, especially, the customer's name if he/she offers it, so you can repeat it back to him/her before the conversation ends.

Listen to peoples' initial request, to get an idea what they are expecting out of our service, or to advise if we even offer the type of service they are asking for.

Take control of the conversation by offering to tell exactly what we would do on one of our routine visits to a customer's home. In this way the customer gets all of the information from us; he doesn't find that when he gets off the phone he forgot to check something.

The professionalism used handling all of our phone calls gave us the edge over the competition. Failing to mention one aspect of our service was also doing a dis-service to our customer. How could a customer possibly know what to ask for? We were sure to include all details for the customer; we got the information we needed and the customer got the information he/she needed, because we controlled the script.

You should plan to make your telephone sales' calls when you are 'up'. Because there are no visual aids, you need that extra energy to communicate enthusiasm over the phone. Tackle your tough calls at peak energy periods.

You should write out all the points of your call that you want to be sure to get covered throughout the conversation. By doing this you can refer back to the list when your conversation gets sidetracked, and you'll also ensure that neither your time nor the listener's time has been wasted.

Also remember nothing is sweeter to one's ear than one's own name; so, as you speak to someone over the telephone, write his/her name down so you can repeat it back to her either during the conversation or when thanking her for the call.

One last thing, when in the position of receiving calls, try to take them as they come in. After six years in the travel industry, I can identify with the problem of being swamped with telephone messages that must be returned at the end of the day. It is a lot easier to make the calls and answer the questions as they come, than it is to try to return all of the messages, and follow through with the requests after hours.

If there had been any way that this could have been done when I was a travel consultant – answering incoming calls as they come in – I would have done so; with clients at my desk continually all day long, after hours seemed to be the only time possible to return these calls.

In any case, messages make for a backlog of work; if at all possible handling your calls as they come in is much less stressful.

Social Media and Email Communication

Much has been written about social media and email protocols. We talked about not being able to see body language when speaking to someone by phone, It is even more difficult to read the tonality of an email or message when you can't see or hear the person at the other end.

Often requests of us via social media are brief (< 140 characters) or use abbreviated words and sentences.

I have always believed *email or text messaging is okay if you want to <u>tell someone</u> something*, but *if you are wanting an <u>exchange back and forth</u>, you are better to speak to the person, either in person or on the phon*e.

Having said this, more and more people are hating to use the telephone (myself included). I much prefer the non-interruption of an email or text communication. Email and text allows me to monitor when I choose to read and respond to my communication requests. They don't interrupt my work, because I don't allow them to interrupt my work. I set aside time every day that I read and respond to my email requests – some people take them throughout the day as they come.

It is up to you to determine how you will monitor your time and communication requests. The nice thing about email and social media messages, we have choice.

We're all Salespeople [Entrepreneurs] Selling Ourselves

An effective listener is the person most likely to succeed. We are all salespersons, or entrepreneurs, selling ourselves, if nothing else. Professional salespeople know that by being an effective listener they can often let the buyer sell himself on their product or service simply by pointing out the items that he has told them interest him/her the most.

Introductions

This leads me to meeting people in person. First of all, when introducing yourself, use both first and last names.

Whether over the telephone, or in person, you say: *Hello, it's Deborah Clarke calling*; or Hello, my name is Deborah Clarke; or, greet the person simply by extending your hand and saying "Deborah Clarke"; of course you must look for the other person to, in turn, introduce him/herself.

You should then repeat this person's name to yourself or out loud, to be sure of accuracy (as well as making it easier to remember once you've said it aloud).

If you meet someone with a difficult name, or if you have a difficult name yourself, it helps to have an easy way for people to remember your name.

One example, a colleague was considering changing his last name for business purposes until we reviewed this technique and he realized being able to help people remember his name made him even more memorable ... his last name was Martynuik; a difficult name to remember and spell. After some coaching he came up with Hi, My name is Matthew Martynuik ... it's like having three first names Matthew Martin and Nick, Matthew Martin-Nick. People easily remembered him after that explanation.

As simple as my name is Deborah Clarke – I'm always adding that's Clarke with an 'e' ... and typically that is how people would remember me ... Deborah Clarke with an 'e'.

How can you make your introduction and name memorable? By helping people associate some part of your name with some kind of memory anchor.

It is important to know people in your presence. It may be to your benefit to acknowledge that presence at a later date.

The Handshake

While referring to a handshake situation I'll also mention that you should shake with a firm, but not knuckle-breaking grip, and try to shake with your hand on the top; this tends to give you more authority or the 'upper hand' (excuse the pun) in the situation.

When introducing other people, rank tends to have its privileges. The order which is most acceptable in the business world is as follows:

Peer to outside peer

A non-official to an official

Junior executive to a senior executive

Fellow executive to a customer

A younger person to an older person (lastly if no other rank applies)

Understanding Acceptable Business Procedures

When you are out in the business world you should treat each situation as an opportunity to allow yourself to shine by being aware of the "acceptable procedures", also by being co-operative, well-prepared, and organized.

In the business world it is your responsibility to make sure your accomplishments are visible. While 'blowing your own horn' may not be your style, it can be done effectively through subtle comments, memos and/or reports, etc. Your aim should be for you to be viewed as someone who is reliable, and whose actions and total image portray nothing less than what would be expected of any professional business person.

Tips

Following are a couple of subtle tips that will help to give you the edge over your customer or peer.

When in restaurants, taverns, etc. always sit in the stiffer chair, rather than the type that you sink down into. Your authority tends to sink down into the chair with you. When you get yourself into this type of situation you tend to have everyone looking down at you and it is difficult to come across with the authority you were hoping to portray.

If you have the option of ordering your own office furniture, you'll be in more control of situations if your chair is elevated even the slightest bit over those of your customers across the desk from you. This of this as being your 'home field advantage'.

Write down everything that requires a follow-up. Don't try to trust your memory. Once on paper, the list becomes more of a commitment.

This also disciplines you to do those things you'd rather not do. For any of you who may be procrastinators, like I used to be, memorize the simple phrase, "Do it now" "Do it now" "Do it now" and repeat it hundreds of times whenever you think of it.

By doing this, your subconscious can again take over and will remind you of that phrase when you have something to do which you really don't want to do. You'll hear that quiet voice inside of you saying, "Do it now!", and of course, you will. It's simple and it works.

Establish a Powerful Image in the Workplace; "getting along with the boss"

Many times, developing a powerful image in the workplace means nothing more than getting along with the boss.

People who are successful in this area usually do the following:

They find ways to learn about the boss's goals, pressures, strengths, weaknesses and working style.

They are aware of their own needs, objectives, strengths, weaknesses, and personal style.

They create a relationship that fits the style and needs of them and their boss.

They continually strive to maintain a good working relationship by keeping their boss informed, by behaving honestly, and by using wisely their boss's time as well as other resources' time.

Establish a Powerful Image in the Workplace; "influence staff and subordinates"

In order to develop the power necessary to influence staff and / or subordinates you must:

Always be honest with them. If you say you are going to do something that affects them directly, follow-through, or have a darn good reason to explain to them why you've been unable to follow through.

Don't have employees do anything that you wouldn't do yourself, and let them know that. Stepping in to give them a hand when necessary is the best way to get this across. There is nothing wrong though, admitting to them that they are better at doing the job than you, because they should be if they do it every day. You know the functions of the duty and / or equipment and can perform a quality job, but they should be capable of doing it more efficiently because of their daily involvement and practice.

You must come across to your employees in the same manner or fashion that you expect them to behave. For example – Don't expect them to constantly be on time and put in a full day's effort if you, yourself, consistently come in late and leave early for no apparent reason.

Show an interest in your employees' welfare, but don't get too involved in employees' after-hours lifestyle. Involve yourself only to the degree that involves work and working conditions.

Set goals for your business or job as you do for yourself.

Share those goals (that you are allowed to share) with the staff. They will feel a sense of belonging when you do, and it also makes them feel proud of their jobs when they see a goal you've set realized.

Chart the growth of your business. Start out by making up either an annual, monthly or weekly graph, (whichever is most feasible for your type of business) and charting out your expected sales, the number of units sold, etc. on this graph.

This becomes a visual set of goals for your employees to follow as you fill in the actual figures. It adds a new dimension to their jobs, give them something visible that they can work towards and something they can judge as their own personal contribution to the company. It tends to give them a sense of belonging, involvement.

Helping other people will help yourself

Remember helping others helps yourself. It is worth giving a lending and whenever we can. And besides, if we all consciously did this – wouldn't our world be a better place to live?

Personally I feel this is one way I can leave my mark in the world; helping someone else to succeed or do well is the best shot in the arm that anyone can give you; it will keep the adrenalin running high. Although, I'm going to mention here that, if you volunteer to do something for someone, follow through and do it promptly.

Networking isn't easy for everyone

Lastly, I've written about the importance of networking and reaching out to others to help us get ahead, this is fine and easy to talk about for some of us – but not so easy for others. Why is it that some people have a harder time than others reaching out for that helping hand?

I believe it all stems from our previous conditioning, sometimes as far back as childhood. Picture this: a little girl, while growing up is handed a doll and told to go play quietly somewhere by herself; while a little brother, however, is handed a hockey stick, baseball bat and glove, soccer ball, etc. and told to go find some friends to play with.

Would it be surprising that, with this type of conditioning bred into these children, the brother would have a much easier time in his adult life approaching business associates and other contacts when he needs help? And yet, the little girl struggles through life just getting by because she subconsciously feels that she must do everything by herself.

She feels that she is expected to learn and work by herself without needing a lot of outside stimulation. I use a girl with a doll, and a boy with a hockey stick as examples – this same conditioning would be relevant if a young boy was expected to sit and play quietly all of the time.

It just seems many adults prompt more aggressive behavior from boys rather than girls – and yes this is still happening. I see it happening with my two daughters all of the time. Knowing this my husband and I became real advocates to get our daughters involved in team sports from a very young age.

It is okay to reach out for help

We have to recognize that it is all right for all of us to reach out and ask for help, as well as offer help back. Life is the same two-way street for everyone. So, even if it feels awkward at first, make the effort to turn to others for assistance.

You'll be surprised at the number of people who want to help you out there, but they don't realize that they have what you want or need.

For example: I used to say to students during career appointments, if you tell me you are *looking for anything* for your first job, <u>I won't think of you</u> because you've done nothing to make yourself stand out.

If you can be more specific (even if you tell different people different things) you have a better chance. For Example: if you like fast or exotic cars and a job comes up with Mercedes Benz Financial, I may think to drop you a line about the opportunity.   If you tell me you eat cereal morning and night, I might think of you for General Mills.

As a business woman *I've never hired someone simply because they were looking for a job,* but if the person can tell me why they like my company, or the work that we do, now they have my attention and it is more likely I will remember them.

All of the things I have just talked about are ways of making ourselves more visible. Visibility is an important avenue to achieving our goals. If we want our goals to happen, we have to go after them, dong so should be fun for us, and the end result should allow you to give yourself a huge pat on the back.

You must work on creating your opportunities – it will take a lot longer, or may never happen if you wait for opportunity to find you.

For More Information: Search "7 Secret Ways To Tap Into The Hidden Job Market For Your Competitive Advantage" in our CareersGettingStarted Blog at
http://www.CareersGettingStarted.com

Also LIKE our FB Page:
http://www.fb.com/CareersGettingStarted

A major accomplishment doesn't come along without several minor accomplishments along the way. Each is a stepping stone which will eventually pave your way to success in achieving your goals. If you plan each step along the way, you'll be more than ready to accept you success, and will appreciate and enjoy it to its fullest.

VISUAL IMAGE –

"Your outer image, does it match your goals?"

> "What you are speaks so loudly, I hardly hear a word you're saying."

Oh, how true it is. I've seen it, I have been manipulated by it in others, and I've used the effect myself.

People can't help judging a book by its cover, and more certainly the majority can't help but be influenced by your appearance, which will leave them with a lasting impression of you, whether right or wrong. It's up to you to make that first impression a good one.

If we view life in general as one big game, it becomes easier to relate to 'the rules', and just as every different sport requires a uniform, so does any situation in life (at least in any situation where you will be judged by others, and whether you like that thought or not, it is almost every day of your life).

The Interview

Take for example an interview situation. You have approximately five seconds when you first walk into a room to be visually accepted or rejected by your interviewer. In that short time the interviewer will have subconsciously decided whether he/she will listen to you or try to rush you back out the door. If we try to remember this example at all times, we will find we'll be better accepted in any situation where we are at our visual best, or in other words in our power look.

So before we go any further with your goal-planning, I suggest you spend some time determining what your power look is going to be. Remembering the marketing strategy, "sell the sizzle, not the steak" should help you to determine what your power look should be. If people think you look confident, (and this goes beyond your wardrobe to the way you carry yourself, your body language, and your accessories), then you will be assumed to be so and at the same time be expected to be competent and interesting.

The First 30 Seconds

In general instances, when we walk into a room, each of us has 30 seconds to make a first impression. Make sure you get your full 30 seconds worth! This is quite often easier talked about than actually done.

Some people seem to have the knack for power dressing, others seem to be born with the inner confidence in themselves which demands the respect of others, and yet others have such an air about them that you are absolutely positive that they must be someone important.

Don't be fooled by the packaging! Anyone can learn the professional business image game. All it takes is a little desire to learn and some research on your part. All it needs to cost you, to learn, is your time and willingness to study the tricks of the trade.

> People see the results of who we are and often judge at the
>
> WINK OF AN EYE:
>
> Our economic level
>
> Our educational level
>
> Our trustworthiness

Our social position

Our level of sophistication

Our success...

And possibly our future.

I'm not suggesting that everyone should be decked out in a navy business suit, white shirt and briefcase (which by the way is the most powerful, stable business look most often used by bankers, insurance people and sales people).

Your power image should be determined by your business interests. This reminds me of a short story that will get the message across.

Every Business / Career has a Uniform

Picture yourself in this situation.

You have boarded an aircraft, sitting prepared for take-off, a half hour passes by and no explanation as to why the aircraft isn't talking off, three quarters of an hour passes and you happen to glance out your window to see a gentleman in a three-piece suit, carrying a briefcase, running towards the plane.

He runs on, jumps in the cockpit, and within five minutes you are hearing him over the loud speaker, "Sorry for the delay ladies and gentlemen, this is your captain speaking."

Do you start to get a little nervous? Right, you get a lot nervous – who is this guy in the airplane that claims he is your pilot? Where is his pilots' uniform and wings?

Just as obvious, if your business falls into the fitness category, then most certainly you should be seen as someone who is always sporty-looking, neat and tidy and very healthy, because that is the sizzle that will sell your business interests.

The 'sizzle' is simply showing others the outcome. People see the results of who we are and often judge, at just the wink of an eye, our economic level, our educational level, our trustworthiness, our social position, our level of sophistication, our success and possibly our future. As much as you may disagree with this, or want to disbelieve it, I'm sorry but the majority of cases it's true and in order to get what you want you may just have to play the game.

Remember the girl in your graduating class whose course average was always above 90%. In a yellow, ruffled dress she may not get a chance to tell her interviewer that she holds an MBA, if she gets weeded out of the waiting room by the secretary because she doesn't look serious enough for the job. Yet the woman with her powerful-looking business suit or dress, who may fall short in the education or experience category, gets an opportunity to at least prove herself simply by being dressed properly for the job.

Imagery, "selling the sizzle, not the steak", is important don't let it be an area you overlook. It will most certainly have some impact on you achieving the goals on your list.

Dress for the Position You Want – Not the Position You Have

If you're working towards a higher position within your company, and wondering why someone else got the job instead of you, I suggest you do some serious research about portraying a more professional image – when the next opening comes up it may be all the information you need to get the job.

Start by taking notice of others in business around you – your competition, your associates, or those currently holding the position you want; assess how they dress, carry themselves, prepare themselves for business, then make sure you are doing the same things yourself, and lots more!

An exercise I've used with clients related to 'money mindset' work is to ADD A ZERO to your current annual salary. Example if you make $40,000 – make your new 'money mindset' salary $400,000. Then ask yourself, as someone who earns $400,000 per year, how would I dress? How would I act? Who would I socialize with? What new connections would I be making? See how this easily shifts the way you think about how you carry yourself and how you project yourself to the world.

Go for the Best Quality You Can Afford

We all remember the girl who was most popular during our high school years as the one who never wore the same outfit twice in a month. Well, in the business world those days have passed, and are out of style. Better quality clothes that work well together and can be mixed and matched, will serve you much better.   You'll be sure that you are always looking your best.

A basic suit of the best quality you can afford will take on several new looks with a couple of different blouses, scarves, etc. for the women; and different shirts, ties, etc. for the men.

Let me share a quote with you that I hung on the wall beside my bed for the entire time I was pregnant with my second child. I knew that I would have to start a new wardrobe after going through two pregnancies in three years.

> "Go for the most expensive clothes you can afford
>
> and you'll always feel proud of the way you look.
>
> It's better to have a few good outfits than a multitude
>
> of cheap ones that will do nothing to enhance your
>
> executive image."

Dress Like a Winner and You'll be Treated Like One!

It has been said that if you dress like a winner – you'll be treated like one. And you can start today!

> "Does your image match your goals?"

Wardrobe is a very personal thing, if you research this topic you'll find as many different opinions as you will find books or consultants. I have found ten basic pieces for men and women that have stood the test of time, these will be a good starting ground for a new business wardrobe.

Best Basic Suit Colors

The best basic suit colors for your wardrobe are Black *, Dark Grey (Charcoal), Navy, or Brown   *My notation for black is that this color is suitable for a women's business suit, but not a man's, a black suit is considered formal wear for gentlemen.

When starting out, build your wardrobe around two major colors, using a third as an accent color.

Your Basic Suit Color Preference

My basic colors

1) _____ ; 2) _____ ;

My accent color   3) _____

A basic mix/match wardrobe for the ladies

TEN BASIC PIECES TOWARDS A NEW BUSINESS
WARDROBE

1) A suit jacket (of your basic color) in a classic line. Three classic styles that come to mind are the standard blazer style jacket with a standard lapel size of approximately 1 ½ inches; the box style suit jacket with no collar, with or without buttons down the front; or the classic style suit jacket with no lapel and one button closing at the waist.

These are the styles that will give you long wear, invest a little more in them, the price in the long run will be a bargain compared to less expensive but trendy styles which may tempt your shopping eye.

2) A matching skirt (of your basic color).
3) A plain color blouse (white, ivory, beige).
4) A printed blouse (part of a two-piece set, which will give you the look of a dress).
5) A printed skirt (part of a two-piece set, to match blouse above, to give look of a dress).
6) Quality dress pant to match suit (in basic color).
7) A blouse patterned with the three main colors in it.
8) A blouse of bold contrasting color.
9) A second jacket (in either second color, or bold contrast color).
10) A sweater, something lightweight that can be worn with all pieces.

A basic mix/match wardrobe for the guys:

TEN BASIC PIECES TOWARDS A NEW BUSINESS WARDROBE

1) A suit jacket (of your basic color) in a classic vs trendy style.
2) The matching suit pants (of basic color).
3) A suit jacket (of your secondary color).
4) The matching suit pants (of your secondary color).
5) A sports jacket for those less formal business arrangements.
6) to 10) Five dress shirts (mix of long sleeved and short sleeved)
   - an assortment of plain white, a light striping; a contrasting color, contrasting collar
   - go for the best quality shirts you can afford … quality is noticed
   -

Of course no business man's wardrobe is complete without a good selection of ties to also mix and match with your two basic suit colors. Then there are shoes … yes, everyone notices your shoes, quality and clean is essential.

For both men and women, once you have established what your major pieces should be, and you have a color scheme to your wardrobe, you can add one or two pieces each season to give it a lift when needed.

With a plan, you can effectively shop at the best quality stores during sale time and get pieces of good quality clothing that will work well with your entire wardrobe. In this way, you too can afford designer brands, and look your very best. Remembering it is the little things that mean a lot, I have listed some tips and suggestions for your consideration:

SUITS

Avoid anything too trendy. Your classic suits, in best quality, will take you many more places, for twice as long. Avoid baggy suits that don't fit properly. A good tailor made-to-fit suit is a real treat and a worthwhile investment for your career. The first time you get to spend $1,000 or more on a good suit, it feels SO AMAZING!

Recognize the difference in looks for the 9:00am-5:00pm versus "after hours". Better known as boardroom versus bedroom looks.

Well-tailored dresses are also acceptable business looks for women.

SHOES

Wear good polished shoes, in leather. People do look at your feet and quality counts.

The definite business shoe for women is a basic pump with a heel that is comfortable for you to walk in. Sling-backs and sandals should be reserved for 'after-hours' although an open-toed pump is acceptable.

This is my best discovery tip yet. In order for women to create the illusion of being tall, try to match the color of your skirt/pants with your hose and shoes. Or try a taupe colored hose, with a taupe colored shoe. Or natural legs with natural colored shoes. This is done so your feet don't stand out, they blend into your leg, giving the illusion of a longer leg. Watch models, you will find a good number of them wear natural colored shoes.

Gentlemen, keep this in mind too, black socks/black shoes; brown socks/brown shoes, grey socks/grey shoes, etc.

PURSES

Purses should always be of good quality. Nothing throws off an entire look faster than a cheap or worn out purse. Watch out for worn straps or tattered looking purses.

LAPTOP or METRO (Messenger) BAGS, BACKPACKS

For the ladies: When I'm travelling, if I have to carry my laptop or iPad I try to carry my wallet in it, so I don't carry a purse and a laptop bag. Keep the few personal things you need to carry hidden inside your laptop bag, hidden from view when you open it. It's best and less cumbersome to carry one or the other (purse or laptop bag), not both.

For the guys: It is acceptable for you to carry either a laptop/metro type bag or backpack to house your laptop when travelling.

My preference for the most professional look for men and women is the laptop or metro bag for business, but I am finding both acceptable for men and women in business.

BELTS

If your suit, or dress outfit comes with a cheap or plastic belt, change it. Get yourself a good selection of leather belts to go with your basic business wardrobe.

BUTTONS

If you want to add some value to the look of a blouse or jacket, put some life back into an older piece of clothing – try changing the buttons. For example, pearl buttons look great on a ladies blouse and add femininity.

HEMLINES

Ladies, find a length that is comfortable for you and stick with it. Without doubt, hemlines change with the trends from year to year. In business, you can't beat the flat panel pencil skirt, with hem just above or at the knee. This is a classic look that has never gone out of style.

Ladies and gentlemen, find the right pant length for all of your pants, with business shoes, and make sure all pants are hemmed when you buy them, or take them to a tailor for proper hemming. Well-proportioned suit jackets, with sleeve length, jacket length and pants hemmed at proper length is essential. Quality in a poor fitting suit doesn't do anything to help you.

SLEEVES

Most acceptable sleeve length for business is long sleeve. If a short sleeve has to be worn, be sure you always have your jacket with you.

NAILS

Fingernails should be kept immaculately clean and trimmed at all times. Ladies nails should be worn ¼ inch above the tip of the finger. Longer nails carry the stigma 'that you don't do anything'. For business, use clear polish, or French tipped nails. Fingernails with chipped polish on them add unnecessary stress to your day.

FRAGRANCE

Perfume and aftershave are very personal choices. For that reason they should be worn with discretion, either very lightly or none at all. Your fragrance choice may offend someone, or perhaps your associate or client is allergic to it. This would definitely put you at a disadvantage, and you don't need to chance that.

BASIC ACCESSORIES**

What does your smartphone case** say about you? Can you proudly set it on the boardroom table? Restaurant table?

necklaces for ladies (short and long)

good selection of ties for men

a good quality watch (business people are always checking the time, so this is a good investment); and yes, even with our smart phones, watches are coming back into vogue.

a laptop bag, or messenger bag for your iPad and connection accessories.

scarves for the ladies

an all-weather, or overcoat / trench coat, is a must for both men and women. The most acceptable colors for business are beige, navy, grey or black.

** Here is a website to check out and share to get some great practical accessories. https://CareersGettingStarted.com

You may agree, or disagree with the basic tips I have just covered. You may also be pondering the term 'business casual' or 'smart casual' that seems to be so prevalent in the business world today.

Make no mistake about it, business casual is still business. In many cases it means, you can leave the jacket at your desk, but guys I'd still be wearing shirt / tie / pants / exceptional shoes. Ladies can be dresses, skirts or pants/top without jackets, again with exceptional shoes.

Don't dress down to jeans unless that is absolutely the 'norm' in the environment that you work.

There is no question in my mind that wardrobe is a very personal thing, but we all must recognize the acceptable business looks. Whether you want to abide by them is up to you – at least be aware of them.

A politician will tell you that his/her audiences respond only 10% to what he/she says; 30% to his/her mannerisms; and 60% to how he/she looks. I think we all should consider the politicians' example for any business encounter.

JUST TWO MORE THINGS:

1) Accept praise gracefully; never make an excuse for your good grooming, wardrobe, or work. Accept praise, don't discount it, simply say: "Thank you"

2) Portray confidence in yourself by looking your best, standing tall, and listening carefully at all times.

Match Outer Image with Inner Goals

I've been trying to point out to you the importance of matching your outer image with your inner goals. If you choose to further your career in the business world, dress in accordance with the position you want, not the position you currently have.

If you think that, as a junior executive, you can get away with wearing the same clothes that you did in high school, college or university because they are good enough for right now, think again. You may never see that senior position unless you are viewed as someone who would 'fit' the role.

One of the hardest things for a person with a senior position to do is inform one of his/her employees that he/she needs to improve as area of personal grooming or wardrobe.

You may have the best job skills, but if you fall short in personal grooming habits, personal cleanliness, or if in any way you don't conform to the expected business image, you will likely not hear about it, and you will be less likely to ever move ahead, and you may never learn why.

Look at the people in the positions you are after, what do they all have in common? View their entire image, visual (clothing, etc), as well as their body language, listening patterns and so on. How are they different from you?

Learning the answers to these questions could be as important as all of your job skills put together.

Don't Fight a Losing Battle …

If your goals see you doing one thing, yet you live and think something completely different, you're fighting a losing battle. Either your goals are important enough to learn more about how must change your way of thinking in order to achieve them, or you must become more realistic with yourself and change your goals.

Don't set goals that aren't important to you, or that aren't worth working for, because you're beating yourself by not allowing yourself to feel the sensation of accomplishment. That is the same sensation that will give you the drive to set further goals and give you the zest for living.

Charisma: What is charisma and how do we get it?

Is it a SKILL or an ATTITUDE?

Allure, appeal, attraction, charm, presence – charisma. What a wonderful word.

I remember a high school English teacher talking to our class about charisma, he was trying to explain just what this phenomenon was. In the end he pointed out that he felt I had charisma, as well as the 'class clown' sitting beside me. At that point I wasn't sure charisma was something I wanted to have. LOL.

Since that time, I've been interested in observing people. What makes one person appear to be more charismatic than another? There is no double people who have charisma, have a marketable edge … so what is it and how do we get it?

> What is the attraction, charm, presence that makes people with charisma different from others?

I'm not sure I have all the answers here for you, but the following is a sampling of what I believe will add to your charismatic powers: (add some ideas of your own)

- *A definite confidence in oneself. Confident but not cocky;*

- *An ever smiling face. (happy demeanor);*

- *An intriguing mystique about them, interesting stories, but they often listen more than they talk, with that 'been there done that' (without having to say anything) sense of satisfaction inside;*

- *Look for the bright side in most situations. (optimism);*

- *Enjoy people, they are interesting, enjoy living. (they're fun to be around);*

- *Inner peace, satisfaction with life.*

- *A presence when you walk into a room. The "You had me at hello" presence.*

Discuss with a friend, or family member whether you feel charisma is a skill or an attitude. Is this something that can be learned?

Action

Chapter 7
Taking the First Step – DREAM

Chapter 8
How to Turn Dreams into Goals

Chapter 9
Performance Management
- Striving for Balance

Chapter 10
On the Road to Success!

Chapter 7

Taking the First Step - DREAM

If life can be compared with a parade there are three types of people:

1) First person is the person marching down main-street in the middle of the parade.

2) Second type of person is the person who stands along-side watching the parade go by.

3) The third type of person 'doesn't even know there is a parade'.

I want you to be the persons marching down main-street - with awareness, enjoying life – in the middle of the parade. Get out there and just do it.

The first step in all goal-setting processes is to identify your "dream", or "vision".

While the business community talks about visions and missions, only a few do this really well. A solid company-wide vision and mission statement understood by everyone empowers employees to own their worth within an organization.

To empower an employee to understand how their contributions help the organization succeed is a very powerful existence.

While many businesses fail in this regard, there is no mistaking professional athletes and performance coaches have understood the power of 'positive visions' and 'dreaming' for years and years.

STORY: I have often thought of the young gymnast Mary Lou Reddon, a USA Olympic Athlete, when I think of visualizing a goal. She openly admitted during interviews following her success at the Olympics that she would lay in bed at night watching herself vaulting over the box-horse and landing a perfect 10. Then she would watch the judges hold up the perfect 10 score cards and she would see her reaction.

As history would have it, she got herself into that exact situation. She would only achieve the gold medal IF she was able to land straight 10 scores across the board with the judges in her final vault. And YES SHE DID!

Canadian, Alwyn Morris, a Mohawk Indian from Quebec, Canada won gold and bronze medals in kayaking at the 1984 Olympics. All Canadians were proud when Alwyn held an eagle feather high over his head while the Canadian National Anthem was played for his gold win. The Kahnawake Reserve put out a poster in his honor. It hung in my office for many years, with large gold print:

> IF YOU HAVE IT IN YOU TO DREAM, YOU HAVE IT IN YOU TO SUCCEED.

In this chapter I have prepared some 'dream sheets' for you to take the first step toward living your dream. In the next chapter you will learn how to turn these dreams into goals. ENJOY.

1. Six month exercise

2. Personality characteristics/traits

3. Limitless exercise

4. 10 year letter to yourself

EXERCISES:

"How to" - The Goal-setting Process

Three exercise templates are included for you to start the goal-setting process. Keep these exercises and final list of top 10 goals, and put them into practice for about six months, then repeat the exercises.

Exercise #1   Six Month Dream Sheet
Write out today's date at the top of the sheet. Across from that write out the date in six months. List all of the things you would like to DO, BE, HAVE in the next six months. This list represents your immediate goals/needs. Review the list of Personality Traits - check off those you would like to work on.

Exercise #2   Limitless Goals
Give yourself a two minute time limit. There are absolutely no limitations to this exercise. Pretend I am a magician, and can give you everything you list on this paper in two minutes - anything you don't write down won't happen in your lifetime. THINK OF EVERYTHING YOU WOULD LIKE TO DO, BE, HAVE AT SOME POINT IN YOUR LIFE. (you have 2 minutes … go!)

Exercise #3   Ten Year Letter to Yourself
Move into the future with this exercise. The year is ten years from today. Write the date at the top of your letter. Address the letter to you - where you would like to be living in ten years? Subject Line RE: Ten year projection letter to me (Today's Date - Date in 10 years).
Dear (first name) (last name):
The first paragraph of the letter should set the scenario for you. How old are you now? How about other family members? What is life like 10 years into the future? What have you been doing for the past 10 years?

Exercise #4   Turn dream sheets into Goals / Complete your Daily Review
Refer to instruction page included. Use visualization techniques.

Dream Sheet – Six Month Exercise

Six Month Exercise	
Today's Date	**Date in 6 months**
_____	_____

(c) D. E. Clarke & Associates "The Business Manager" 1989

Personality Traits Check-List

Check off as many traits as you would like to improve. These will become positive affirmations you can repeat to yourself daily.

	I pursue my goals free of any feelings of ill-will or animosity toward others. I am a warm, friendly, well-liked person. My success is assured and does not require me to take advantage of any other person. It obliges me to help others, without telling anyone about my 'good deeds'.
	I see myself with the success-eye of now. I have discarded the failure-eye of my infancy. I am free at last of failure or limitations.
	I always work on things that count. When I have an enterprise in hand, I concentrate upon it wholly. In my concentration, the rest of the world cannot disturb me.
	I always achieve the desired result, with minimum of time and energy.
	I have completely relaxed self-assurance; I am sure of myself in all situations, and with all people.
	I respect myself and my goals and have complete self-assurance in all that I think and do. I am equal to the best of human beings and truly am capable of great accomplishment.
	I am honest with myself and therefore with everyone else.
	I am well organized in every phase of my life.
	I read quickly and easily with great comprehension of all subject matter.
	I treat all problems as opportunities to be creative, and as a result my life is vastly enriched. I use creativity in every endeavour and thus enjoy a position of growing leadership.
	I have an excellent memory, not only for the immediate tasks but for all experiences that I have had. It grows better every day.
	I am quickly decisive in all matters, only making sure that I have completely accurate data before acting.
	My goals are high, and I reach them easily and quickly by affirming

	them constantly. I am dynamic, in my self-improvement because I am consistent in my efforts.
	I have complete composure at all times. I accept challenge and arguments calmly and in good spirit.
	I meet people easily and enjoy each new association. My deep sincerity puts people at ease and stimulates their confidence.
	I work for quality. I have the patience to do simple things perfectly and thereby strengthen my skills to do difficult things easily.
	I know that leaders are readers. I systematically study books and magazines which increase my earning power.
	I successfully train others to do my work. I give those who help me generous credit for their accomplishments. The willing support of other people is essential to my success.

Dream Sheet – Limitless Exercise

Limitless Exercise
Today's Date:
2 Minutes - List Everything you want to DO, BE, HAVE in your lifetime ... NO LIMITATIONS.

10 Year Letter To Myself

Today's Date: _____

Today's date is 10 years into the future.

Dear (Your Name):

Clarke

Chapter 8

How to Turn Dreams to Goals

You are your own vehicle to success; by drawing your own personal road map, knowing your predetermined destination and ETA (estimated time of arrival) all you have to add is desire as the gas to get you there.

Life is a very precious gift. Each new day is the first day of the rest of your life. It is up to you to enjoy it to its fullest. In order to do that and to be able to enjoy the feeling of success and accomplishment, you must first have a plan. It's like taking a road trip anywhere; it's hard to get there without a map.

It seems that everyone to whom I talk acknowledges goal-setting, and agrees upon its importance; many lead me to believe they are also goal-setting people, yet if I challenge them by questioning whether or not they actually sit down and write out their goals and life plans, I find that only a rare few actually do. Are we too modest to even admit to ourselves on paper what we actually want to achieve in life?

Are we afraid someone else might find and read out list of goals and ridicule it? (by the way, your list of goals should be kept confidential, not revealed even to your spouse to avoid any negative input that may hinder your subconscious in believing you can achieve it.) Are we afraid if we put our goals, dreams, and wishes on paper we are setting ourselves up to fail? On the contrary - BY PLANNING AHEAD YOU ARE PLANNING TO WIN!

By painting a clear picture of your wants and needs you are setting yourself up to achieve them, and faster than you ever thought possible. You will be amazed at how things have a way of working themselves out. Things just start happening!

So, if you have been too proud or modest to actually sit down and work through this goal-setting process, now is the time to take a more serious look at goal-setting and get started right now, today.

If you think that so and so, who's president of a big company, or what's his name who is CEO of another company, have become big time achievers by just floating along through life - think again! I haven't met one successful person who can say "I didn't plan it, this just happened." All extremely successful individuals have a very clear outline of exactly what they are after in life, and it is time you did too. Give goal-setting a chance. Once you have a taste of how it will help you along through life, I can guarantee you'll never want to stop.

I'll tell you how I got started, at the age of 19, then by reading on you can work through the steps to develop your own 'master plan'.

Up until the age of 18 my goals were set for me, the same way most goals are set for teenagers today. As I went through the school system, decisions on classes, courses, exams, were made by teachers, and parents. Major decisions concerning my life were, of course, made by me.

At the age of 18 I was out working on my own. By the age of 19 I knew I had to start making some clearer plans of what lay ahead for Deb Clarke. I took a keen interest in goal-setting procedures, read lots of books and put myself through some exercises much like I've had you do.

The first time I put this process into practice was March 1979, five months before I was to get married. My husband and I were living in a one bedroom apartment, driving a 'new' 1978 Cutlass Supreme. Both of us were working although my husband wasn't really happy with where he was working at the time, but it was a job for him. I was in my second year in the travel industry and I knew I had many years ahead of me in the travel business.

In point form, some of my goals that were written out at that time were:

- to own our own home once we got married

- to have a touchtone microwave

- to have a dishwasher (but not before my microwave)

- to have a dog to complete our family for the time being

- to someday see my husband in a career that he would be proud of and from which he could look forward to retirement income

- to eventually supervise the travel agency I was employed in and become a respected agent within the city and industry

- to own a fur coat

I was faithful to the system of reviewing my goals twice a day for approximately one month, then for one reason or another I got away from reading them. In November 1982, three years later, I came across the list; it was mostly in point form like I've shown you, and not in a lot of detail, but I still got the message loud and clear - it was working!

By this time we were married and living in a brand new model home; we had a small house dog; my husband had been laid off from his job just six months after we had purchased our home. You can imagine how devastated we were with the main mortgage earner out of work. But it resulted in him getting a job with an international oil company which he has always admired and respected. He has hoped that one day he might work for this company - now he was. We owned a touchtone microwave, a good used dishwasher, I had been appointed supervisor of the travel agency and had built quite a sizeable clientele; and I had just purchased a coyote fur jacket for myself (April 1982).

Quite frankly, I had amazed myself. How could I have predicted all those things happening three years earlier?

Simply put, my subconscious was given a list of things to do and over that period of time the majority of them had been accomplished. Needless to say, from that day forward I have used goal-setting techniques for all aspects of my life (personal goals, family goals, business goals)

When looking back now - my original list seems extremely incomplete; like anything else, the longer you work at something the better you'll become.

I also believe I mislead people somewhat about the ease of setting goals. The exercises I had you complete in the last chapter (Dream Sheets) are called dream sheets because that is all they really are. Many people think that by writing these thoughts down they have set goals.

Don't get me wrong, it's a start, but to establish firm goals much more detail is needed.

TURNING DREAMS INTO GOALS

Be like a fisherman, pick out those goals most important to you at this time and throw the others back. If your list is rather short, I want you to cast out into deeper waters and search for everything, or anything that you'd ever want to do, be or have. You don't have to limit yourself to any specific number of things. You will eventually have them all, but I don't want you wasting your energy on goals that aren't really important to you.

Once you have your 10 visions in mind, the next step is to find out as much information as you can about that type of achievement. How was it done before? Who did it? Do your homework, find out as much information from other sources as possible.

When your homework / research is completed, re-write your new goal in positive, completed form. Make it sound as though you have already accomplished this goal.

Visualization is a powerful tool when used correctly; it is not daydreaming, or fantasizing - it is getting a clear and detailed image for your subconscious to believe.

Five Tips for Effective Visualization:

1) Picture your goal in the present tense. See it happening now.

2) Keep your picture in the first person: "I" am doing this. If a Hawaiian holiday is one of your goals, don't visualize the beach - see yourself on the beach.

3) You can't visualize the absence of something. If it is a negative you want to correct - you have to visualize the positive you want to happen.

4) Make your visualization as detailed as possible. Sense the image, colors, sounds, and even smell - make it a techni-color movie. If it is a dim picture, brighten it up.

5) And lastly, make sure it is something you really want. Visualization gives certainty to a goal; if you have trouble visualizing your goal, perhaps it is not as important to you as you think.

The biggest hurdle you have to cross is to know and understand exactly what it is you really want. This list will become your list of immediate goals, things you have placed in highest importance, to be achieved first.

Be sure to include the time element - when will this goal be achieved?

Dream, then research your dream. What does it take to make the dream happen? This is the stage the actual 'goal' starts to develop. Then of course you establish your own personal 'plan' and time frame to achieve this goal.

You may have people say to you, "oh, that positive thinking stuff - it doesn't really work". This is more than positive thinking.

- This is positive feelings and your feelings do have a great effect on you and what you do.
- This is research to determine if it is something you really want to do, something you are willing to commit to doing.
- This is training your subconscious to work with you, not against you.
- This is owning up to the control you have over your life.
- This is to make a positive difference in your life and the lives of people who are around you.

Put aside unfavorable comments and let other people think what they want. You are the one who has nothing to lose, but a great deal to gain!

Chapter 9

Performance Management -

Strive for Balance in Your Life

This chapter was added in the 1990 revision of Live Your Dream. It was after working with the original book (c) 1987, and delivering hundreds of workshops that this model emerged.

There is a tremendous difference between a person working at maximum levels of performance and a person working at optimum levels of performance.

Maximum Levels of Performance

The person working at maximum levels will work to achieve his/her goal at any cost. EG. Health, family, personal integrity, etc.

Optimum Levels of Performance

The person who works at optimum levels will work to the best of his/her ability, within the lifestyle he wishes to live.

In my mind, the person who works at maximum levels of performance will achieve short term success. Yes, he/she may achieve goals earlier, faster, but in the long run I've seen too many cases of personal unhappiness. The price of working to the 'max' can be extremely costly.

The person who works at optimum levels of performance is more likely to achieve long term success and personal happiness, satisfaction, peace of mind. This makes optimum performance much more attractive.

> Strive for that optimum balance in your life and success will be sure to come your way, and will stay.

I've had people talk to me after my 'performance management' workshops and say 'you are different', they continue to explain that most performance lecturers preach maximum performance ... with a narrow focus rather than a complete lifestyle focus.

What makes one person more successful than another? What is the difference between the person making $25,000 per year and someone making $250,000 per year (besides the obvious $225,000)? Is the person making $250,000 a year 10 times smarter than the person making $25,000 per year? Not likely. Take this example one step further. What about the person making $2.5 million dollars per year. Is that person 100 times smarter than the person making $25,000 per year? It is physically impossible, I'm told, to be 100 times smarter than another person. So what is the difference?

There is more material on the market today than ever before about success, achievement, performance, etc. But compare this new material with some of the oldest books available and you'll find the underlying message is the same. There are two basic criteria for all success:

- Make a decision to accomplish more (attitude)
- Learn how (skill)

In reverse, there are two reasons why people fail
- Lack of capabilities (skill)
- Lack of personality (attitude)

The majority of people who fail, fail because they don't have the right attitude, they don't adjust to new circumstances.

Go back to Chapter 3 - and revisit the Most Successful Person You Know exercise to reinforce this very point.

Performance Management in Motion

Take a close look. Learn how this model can relate to you personally, or to any given business situation.

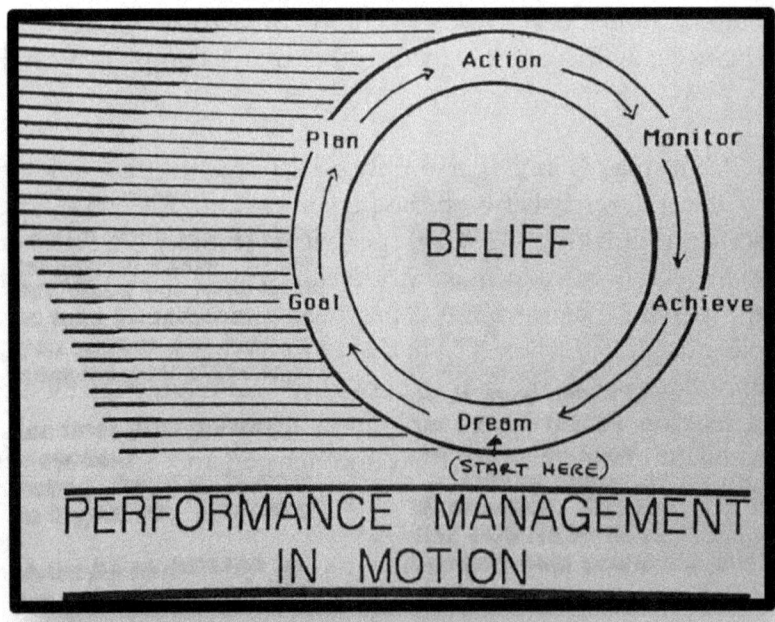

My performance management model, 1990, follows the same Skills/Attitude theory discussed above. The middle of the circle, or core, represents YOU. Your belief in yourself, your company, products. It is essential for both your family and your business associates to be aware of your core beliefs and values. This core very much represents your own personality / attitude.

Once you have made a decision to accomplish more, or to change a behavior, to process of learning how, via the process in the outer circle becomes easier. The process of learning how is essential for your success, but secondary to your own thoughts, attitudes about achieving your goals/objectives.

Take a closer look. Learn how the performance model relates to your business situation.

Belief

(make a decision - attitude)
This represents belief in yourself, your company and your products/service. This is something you have to come to grips with yourself. No one else can decide your basic beliefs/values.

Outer Circle

(process - learning how)
Skills to develop, read on ... start at the Dream stage of the circle.

Dream

(dream / vision)
Athletes have used the inner power of vision for ages. The business world is starting to recognize the benefits of common vision. The reason this inner power works, is our minds think in pictures. If you have it in you to dream, you have it in you to succeed. Don't accept mediocrity, dream. See yourself winning.

Goal

This is the research stage. What does it take to make this vision (dream) or objective happen? Research, research, research. Find out what it has taken for someone else to do what you want to do. It is during this stage you will determine based on your research done, if you want to make this dream a reality, or not. It is okay, once done your research to determine this is no longer something you want to pursue as a goal. A good example here is saying you'd like to lose 10 pounds. Figure out what would be necessary for you to make that happen, and if you are not willing to do what is required to make that happen, stop talking about it. If you do not want to do what is necessary to make your goal happen, change the goal - or drop it.

Plan

This is the stage when you develop your personal plan of attack. In the goal/research stage you have found what it would take for someone else to do what you want to do. Now you have to personalize your objectives, ambitions. This plan becomes your personal blueprint for success. It is worth noting, that it is OKAY to be you ... do it your way (whatever it may be). This PLAN must be ad detailed as possible. Not only what you want to do/be/have, but how are you going to do it.

Action

There are three types of people in this world.
1) People marching in the parade;
2) People watching the parade go by;
3) People who don't even know there is a parade.
If life can be compared to a parade, we all must strive to be the doers, the people marching down the middle of the street in the parade.

Nothing happens until someone takes action. JUST DO IT! Grab a coach** if you need help to get started eBizCoach.ca

***I would be happy to help you as your <u>Online Life Coach</u> – take a look at the Live Your Dream Success Package and see what you can accomplish working with me in just 30 days!*
http://www.ebizcoach.ca/LYD-Plus-Success-Package

Monitor

We all know people (maybe ourselves) who seem busy all the time. They are busy, be we're not sure what it is they are busy doing. Take the time to monitor your progress, your daily workloads ... Ask yourself: "Am I having fun yet?" Two important theories in the monitoring stage. First, look for incremental improvements. Many of our goals will not be achieved tomorrow, next week, or next month, so we must look for milestones to measure our progress. Give yourself credit where it is due, it keeps you focused, on track and stimulated. Second, give yourself NO EXCUSE TO LOSE. Listen to the nagging voice inside your head warning you of trouble ahead. Make note of these warnings and act on them when necessary. Before we even know the outcome we often have our 'excuse' ready in our heads. "If this happens, I'll have this excuse; and if that happens, I'll have that excuse.", etc. Listen to the little voice in your head, think of it as your best friend. Give yourself no excuse to lose.

Achieve

Last, but certainly not least, feel / acknowledge your achievements. Not only in a proud way, to make you feel better, but to appreciate what you already have. Be thankful of your progress and accomplishments. There aren't enough people in this world to give us the pats on the back that we need. Learn to quietly recognize your achievements, feel the satisfaction. Then move on. ..

Chapter 10

On the Road to Success

Extra effort got you where you are today.
Working smarter will get you where you want to go tomorrow.
Remember, the only security you have is in yourself. Enjoy.

Live Your Dream puts you in the drivers' seat: your destination is happiness and fulfillment in life. Congratulations! Having made it this far through the book, you are well on your way to success. It feels good to be in control, 'in the drivers' seat', doesn't it!

The greatest fear most people have is fear of the unknown, but if you have a clear path / insight to where you are going and ideas about how you're going to get there, then all that's left if handling any roadblocks and obstacles as they come up. that challenge is what keeps us striving - once you accept that there will be some setbacks, and you will make some mistakes along the way - you can turn those setbacks and mistakes into strengths for you.

Robert Frost summed up fearing and the unknown in his poem, "The Road Not Taken"

> Two roads diverged in a wood, and I
>
> I took the one less travelled by,
>
> and that has made all the difference.

Every time a new problem or new set of circumstances came up in my previous business, I used to tell the ladies in my employ,

"Part of being professional is being able to handle all situations calmly. Now that we have learned how to handle this situation the next time if it happens again, we'll be able to handle it even more professionally as we will be prepared."

You have to face problems in order to become well-versed and able to handle them another time. While I was a supervisor in the travel industry, when a seemingly drastic problem was brought to my attention I used to tell staff, 'there is a solution to every problem - be calm - we'll work it out." I still believe and live by this. I have never come across a problem that some kind of solution hasn't been able to resolve.

So my point here is, if the only fear (or at least the worst one) is of the unknown, and we are willing to face that with great courage, nothing should be standing in the way of our path to success.

Throughout this book, you have learned to:
1. Identify your true values and determine your meaning of success
2. Make detailed lists of your goals; along with tips on how to work that list.
3. Use techniques available at little or no cost, to improve the way you come across professionally and to assist you in achieving your goals.

All of these are strategies to be aware of when pursuing your 'business of successful living'.

I suggest that you start a binder for all of your goal-setting notes so that you can accumulate them over the years. Title it, "My Personal Success Strategies". In the front half of the binder include this, your first set of serious goals and goal-setting techniques. Keep adding pages as you accomplish your goals. It is fun to review your lists periodically and to write in the dates you achieved what you were after. It'll knock your socks off to see how successful you really are! In the second half of the binder I suggest you keep a journal of all of your business activities, Eg. training courses, certificates, other achievements and dates. You never know when your 'secure for life' job may come to an end, and sometimes it is hard to remember (after many years) all that you really have accomplished. If you keep track, you won't short-change yourself.

> NOTE: If you would like to take a 'deeper dive' into this material with **30 days of personal online coaching** and exercises with Deborah … for very little financial investment – go to **http://www.ebizcoach.ca/lyd-plus-success-package** Tell me why you'd like to work with me, I'd love to help you discover your next success story.

Something I'd like to leave you with, as you are well on your way to achieving your success, is some thought about ways you can assist someone else early in his or her career.

I believe strongly in the words taken from Whitney Houston's song, The Greatest Love of All. "I believe that children are our future. Teach them well, and let them lead the way. Show them all the beauty they possess inside, give them a sense of pride."

I believe it is our responsibility to help new leaders develop and follow in our footsteps.

The checklist on the next page is a handful of ways we can pay-it-forward and help new young graduates find their way in their careers too: Use this checklist yourself and share it freely!

Ready To Adopt A Pay-It-Forward Attitude?

Ways We Can Help New Graduates Manage Their Careers During The Early Stages.

Start by:

- Introducing young people to career fields that fit their interests, values, skills, and strengths (remember the value of Information Interviews);

- Teaching them the leverage that is provided by developing relationships, knowledge, skills, track record, etc. early on the job;

- Making them understand that they should not measure their entire career progress by pay raises and promotions alone, but rather by monitoring more appropriate measures of performance and personal growth;

- Helping them to develop one important source of power in their field of work, it could be a relationship with a mentor, a coach, a sponsor;

Capable young people who are entering the job market for the first time rarely have a clear sense of who they are, their limitations, and their own real strengths and weaknesses. After being automatically promoted every twelve months in school for most of their lives, many over-estimate what they can do and where they can be both successful and happy.

Others, especially those who have not had good role models at home and in school, usually recognize that they are not as good at one subject as they are at another but that information does not translate easily into specific occupational advice: it only gives them general guidance.

Consider sharing a copy of Live Your Dream with someone.

My suggestions to young people assessing a first career choice include 7 Key Success Factors (KSF):

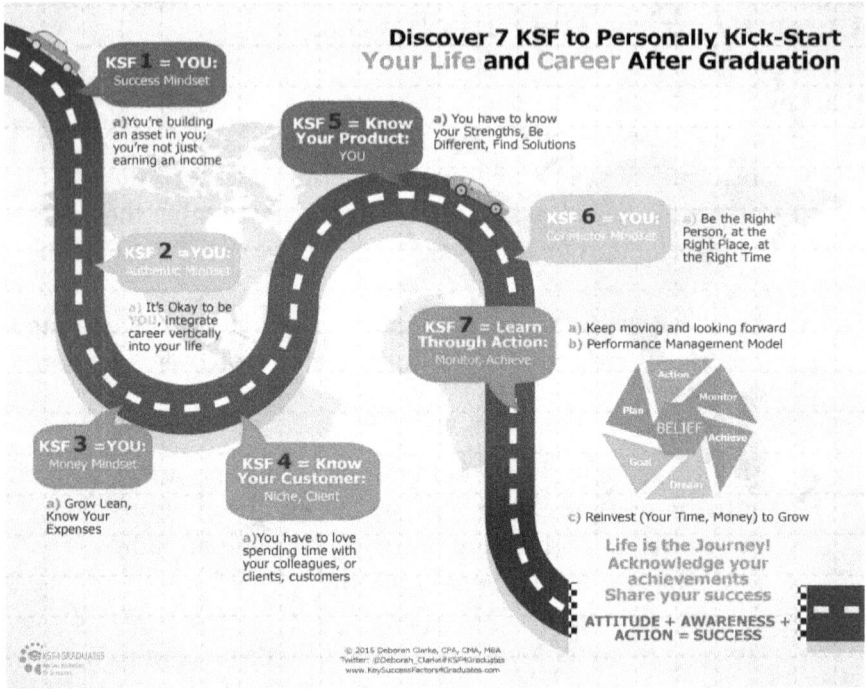

I always start by asking new graduating students:

1) _Geographically_ where do you want to live?

2) What _Industries_ are you most interested in?

3) What are the **_top 3 Companies_** in the industry you like, in that geographic region? Learn all you can about these top 3 companies.

If you would like to help a new graduate figure out 'what's next after graduation' – or to read more about the 7 KSFs, please go to:
http://www.ebizcoach.ca/ksf4graduates-course/

My Final Words of Wisdom

Achievers are made, not born. As obvious as this may seem, I remind you the average person can accomplish 40-50 percent more than he or she thinks he can.

Achievers keep themselves busy, competing not with others but with themselves. Remember, your goals are dreams with research and deadlines.

The top achievers see themselves not only at the height of their success, but more importantly, at every plateau along the way.

Achievers trust their own intuition, and often go with their gut feelings.

As you finish reading this book, I hope I have furnished you with the tools needed for you to learn how to fish on your own.

I urge you to ask yourself: (Author unknown)

"Do I want to settle for the big nothingness of the middle road?
Or, do I want to try for the top, take risks, and do something important?
Do I want my life to be productive, exhilarating and enriching - an
adventure?
If your answer is yes, then you've got to go out there and take risks,
for without the element of risk and chance, life is dull.
Fulfillment, excitement, and happiness await you if you
let every summit to be a valley to a peak beyond."

From the Author in Closing

Set your ambitions high, as I have, and you will reap the rewards of your choice.

A freelance writer who interviewed me for a business magazine summed up my ambitions by saying:
"An old proverb for success says: She saw an occasion and riz to it. and that's all there is to it. In Clarke's case, that's not all there is to it. There are goals to be set and re-set with the same confidence that tells her the sun will shine tomorrow, and the next day and the next."
> - Quote by Hope Morritt, Sarnia Business Trends
> Magazine, February 1985.(God rest her soul)

[1991 revision, D. Clarke] "I'm still aiming high ... I'm still learning ... I'm still growing ... but most of all I'm enjoying life, and taking the time to appreciate what we (as a family) already have.
I wish all of the same happiness and inner peace for you. Don't take life for granted - take charge. LIVE YOUR DREAM, and enjoy!"

[2015] The original 1987 book (with 1989 and 1991 revisions) was republished as an **e-book on Amazon. The original Live Your Dream** book lives again! As you know the research and original writing of Live Your Dream was done when I was between the ages of 26-28. Go To Amazon – Search *Live Your Dream Deborah Clarke*

[2017] Live Your Dream has been given an overhaul. I hope you enjoy this new version. It's now available as an eBook and also in paperback. My goal is to help you find that elusive something that will lead you to success and happiness. I hope we have done that with Live Your Dream, 2017. If you would like to dive deeper into these exercises with 30 days of online life coaching with Deborah – please register at http://www.ebizcoach.ca/lyd-plus-success-package or email me at deborah@ebizcoach.ca Cheers!